HOOKED RUG LANDSCAPES

ANNE-MARIE LITTENBERG

Virginia P. Stimmel, Editor
photographs by Anne-Marie Littenberg

DEDICATION

This book is dedicated to Ben Littenberg,
my constant source of
love, support, and inspiration.

Copyright© 2009 by Stackpole Books

Published by
STACKPOLE BOOKS
5067 Ritter Road
Mechanicsburg, PA 17055
www.stackpolebooks.com

Printed in Fulton, Missouri

First edition

10 9 8 7 6 5 4 3 2 1

Cover photos by Anne-Marie Littenberg
Cover design by Caroline Stover

Library of Congress Cataloging-in-Publication Data

Hooked Rug Landscapes / Virginia P. Stimmel, editor; photographs by Anne-Marie Littenberg.—1st ed.
   p. cm.

  ISBN: 1-881982-65-3;
  978-1-881982-65-4
Canadian GST #R137954772.

CONTENTS

ACKNOWLEDGEMENT

I want to acknowledge my mother, Antje van Klei Pijper, for the background she provided that ultimately led to my pursuit of rug hooking. A single mom with six kids, she worked two jobs and made sure we always had art books on the shelves and Van Gogh prints on the walls. She took me to the Metropolitan Museum of Art in New York City when I was a little girl, and the Van Gogh Museum in Amsterdam when I was 18.

She gave me my first embroidery project before kindergarten (it was a scene of Mary Had a Little Lamb), and taught me to sew my first skirt at age 9. A master tailor and a magnificent quilter, my mother is a miracle.

ABOUT THE AUTHOR

Anne-Marie Littenberg is a self-taught fiber artist. A frequent contributor to *Rug Hooking* magazine, her teaching engagements have included classes at Sauder Village in Archbold, Ohio, and the Green Mountain Rug Hooking Guild's workshops at Shelburne Museum, Vermont. Her hooked rugs have been "viewer's choice" selections at Shelburne and Sauder Village, and her work has exhibited at the Warren Kimble Gallery in Brandon, Vermont, the Remsenburg Academy in New York, and the Ginza Mikimoto Gallery, Tokyo, and a variety of other venues. Her 9 *of Hearts* rug is part of the Art of Playing Cards exhibit. Anne-Marie is past president and past treasurer of the Green Mountain Rug Hooking Guild. She can be contacted at *amwlittenberg@comcast.net*.

A Walk (triptych), #3 of three 36" x 32" panels, #3- to 6-cut recycled and over-dyed wool on linen. Designed and hooked by Jen Lavoie, Huntington, Vermont, 2006.

INTRODUCTION

Why do we hook rugs? For some, it is a hobby. For others, it is a craft related to interior design. For me, it is a medium for artistic expression. And yet, I am struck by how many rug hookers say they are not artists, even though their fine work is original, and their devotion to established methods is firmly rooted in years of study, trial and error.

My goal in writing "Hooked Rugs Landscapes" is to provide rug hookers with tips and tricks of design that have been used in the world of "fine art" for centuries. One could argue that if I'm so interested in fine art, why don't I take up painting instead of rug hooking? The subtle effects achieved by painters with a brush and pig-

ments are mesmerizing to me, and yet I feel compelled to work with fiber. I am drawn to the sensual aspects of the materials; how they look, feel and smell, depending on their composition and weave. Silk snags on the tiniest cracks of my fingers. The scent of wool can be overpowering on a hot, humid day. I hook because I have a visceral urge to, and playing with paint has never appealed in the same way.

As rug hookers, we can take advantage of knowledge and techniques applied to other media in pursuit of our personal artistic vision. Experiment with new color palettes and design ideas. I urge you to be fearless as you create your own hooked rug landscape.

Hinesburg, Vermont, 32" x 25", #6- and 8-cut over-dyed and as-is wool on monk's cloth. Designed and hooked by Rae Harrell, Hinesburg, Vermont, 2002; from the collection of Ramsey Yoder.

FROM THE EDITOR

Throughout history, landscapes have been captured by a wide variety of media—paintings, watercolors, medieval tapestries, and prints, etc. Rug hooking landscapes are a relatively new form of artistic expression. The rugs you will see in *Hooked Rug Landscapes* are a departure from the 18th-century traditional hooked rugs that were utilitarian in design and were made primarily to cover bare floors and ward off the chill.

One of the most popular requests of rug hookers today is how to design and hook realistic landscape rugs. Nothing beats the beauty of capturing a creation of nature and being able to interpret it for a hooked rug pattern. Author Anne-Marie Littenberg breaks down the process with easy-to-follow information plus tips and recommendations on how to achieve your goal. In this book, she discusses not only the inspiration behind your rug, but also how to determine perspective, choose what elements to include, depth perception, color planning—everything you need to create your rug from start to finish.

For a good look at what rug hookers are doing with yesteryear's craft, pick up a copy of *Rug Hooking* magazine or visit our web site at *www.rughookingmagazine.com*. Within the world of rug hooking and *Rug Hooking* magazine, you'll find a style to suit every taste and a growing community of giving, gracious fiber artists who will welcome you to their gatherings.—*Ginny Stimmel*

ABOUT THE PUBLISHER

Rug Hooking magazine welcomes you to the rug hooking community. Since 1989 *Rug Hooking* has served thousands of rug hookers around the world with its instructional, illustrated articles on dyeing, designing, color planning, hooking techniques, and more. Each issue of the magazine contains color photographs of beautiful rugs old and new, profiles of teachers, designers, and fellow rug hookers, and announcements of workshops, exhibits, and gatherings.

Rug Hooking has responded to its readers' demands for more inspiration and information by establishing an inviting, informative website at *www.rughookingmagazine.com* and by publishing a number of books on this fiber art. Along with how-to pattern books, *Rug Hooking* has produced the competition-based book series *Celebration of Hand-Hooked Rugs*, now in its 19th year.

The hand-hooked rugs you'll see in *Celebration of Hand-Hooked Rugs XIX* represent just a fragment of the incredible art that is being produced today by women and men of all ages. For more information on rug hooking and *Rug Hooking* magazine, call or write to us at the address on the copyright page.

CHAPTER 1

What Is A Hooked Rug Landscape?

A landscape represents an artist's perception of the world out of doors. Elements in nature are depicted how the artist chooses to see them. A landscape may be created from a wide variety of subjects and a myriad of media. Cave paintings in France dating back thirty thousand years show the drama of a hunt. Medieval tapestries, woven of the finest wool and silk, illustrate a warrior ruler's travels through the countryside. Lush flora may be depicted in breathtaking accuracy.

Camelshump, 19" x 27", various plied threads of linen, silk, cotton, polyester, wool, etc. on rug warp. Designed and hooked by Anne-Marie Littenberg, Burlington, Vermont, 2003. The profile of the distant mountain depicts Camelshump, one of the Green Mountains. The rest of the composition is imaginary.

Too Cold to Skate, 60" x 36", hand-cut over-dyed wool on rug warp. Designed and hooked by Jule Marie Smith, Ballston Spa, New York, 1994. Jule's primitive rug brings to mind idealized images of rural village life, reminiscent of the compositions of Grandma Moses.

Red Barn with Birches, 26" x 19", #4- and 6-cut hand-dyed and as-is wool on monk's cloth. Designed by Maryanne Lincoln. Hooked by Betty Bouchard, Richmond, Vermont, 2004.

Realistic fauna (horses or dogs) and imagined creatures (unicorns) add to the drama of the story. The prints of Currier and Ives and paintings of Grandma Moses romanticized otherwise mundane activities of American village and coun-try life. French Impressionist painters celebrated the emotional effects of vibrant color and light, rather than accuracy of representation.

While mankind's interpretations of landscapes have existed in various forms

for tens of thousands of years, rug hooking is a relative newcomer to the world of artistic expression. The goal of *Hooked Rug Landscapes* is to teach you how to combine the craft of rug hooking with basic art and design skills that have been used for centuries in other media such as paintings and tapestries.

How do you achieve a sense of depth in a hooked rug? What tricks can you employ to depict a receding horizon? How are color, contrast, and perspective manipulated to create a mountain range, sky, or body of water in a hooked rug?

Use rug hooking techniques to depict landforms, living elements, and more abstract characteristics such as light and weather conditions. Create your own unique vision through your hooked rug art. Try your hand at expressing your personal sensibility and style. You may be surprised by your rug hooking abilities when you work outside your usual comfort zone, exploring new design techniques and color palettes.

The Chicken Whisperer, 24" x 29", #3-cut over-dyed and hand-dyed wool on linen. Designed and hooked by Robin Garcia, Calais, Vermont, 2007.

CHAPTER 2

Inspiration: Selecting a Subject

I am drawn to the spare, transcendent beauty of vast spaces. I find peace in watching the sun set or in seeing moonlight glint on water. I love to hook rugs where the viewer's eye is drawn to the drama of light. I try to create scenes that evoke feelings. My subject may be of secondary importance to the mood or atmosphere created by the design. *Let's Play in the Moonlight*, was inspired by a walk on the rocky shore of Lake Champlain, with the Adirondack Mountains glowing in the distance. Is this rug about the sky and water, the relationship between the person and dog playing on the beach, or romantic ideals about the night of a full moon?

For your landscape, you may choose from an enormous variety of subjects. Do you want to depict a scene of wild natural splendor, evoking the sublime and beautiful? Landscapes often illustrate man's relationship with the land. For instance, a field of corn or a city skyline shows how man has manipulated the land to serve his needs, substantially altering the natural terrain. Perhaps you are more interested in a visceral reaction to a landscape. Sunrise over a mountain may depict a familiar moment of natural spectacle. Landscapes can be used to accent a story. The Garden of Eden is the setting for the Old Testament story of Adam and Eve. An old barn with a mountainous backdrop can record your own family history.

Let's Play in the Moonlight, 49" x 29", various plied threads of linen, silk, cotton, polyester, wool, etc. on verel. Designed and hooked by Anne-Marie Littenberg, Burlington, Vermont, 2005; from the collection of Sharon Townsend.

The Girl on a Rock, 29" x 39", #3- to 6-cut recycled and over-dyed wool on linen. Designed and hooked by Jen Lavoie, Huntington, Vermont, 2003. This rug is based on an old family photo of Jen as a girl.

The Apple, 25" x 32", #6- and 8-cut over-dyed and as-is wool on monk's cloth. Designed and hooked by Rae Harrell, Hinesburg, Vermont, 2002. The landscape of the Garden of Eden is the setting for this Old Testament story.

What subject, set outdoors, would you like to hook? Are you interested in recording a particular event that stands out in your memory? Is there an old family photograph you would like to use as the basis of a design for your hooked rug? Jen Lavoie's *Girl on a Rock* is a self portrait based on a photograph taken when she was a girl.

Are you moved by the memory of a beloved place? Stephanie Ashworth Krauss designed and hooked *Vermont State House* for a resident of Montpelier (Vermont's capital) who is proudly devoted to his hometown. Does your imagination dance with your own ideas of how to illustrate a story, myth, or legend? Betty Bouchard's *Christmas Scene* shows the Star of Bethlehem

The Vermont State House, 34" x 24", #4-, 6-, and 9-cut as-is and over-dyed wool on linen. Designed and hooked by Stephanie Ashworth Krauss, Montpelier, Vermont, 2003; from the collection of Les Matkowski. Note how value and directional hooking help to distinguish the tree foliage on the right from the mountain backdrop.

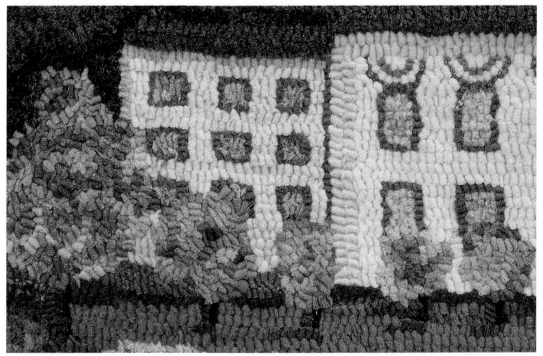

The Vermont State House (detail). Trees line up in front of the State House. The foliage is hooked in rounded swirls, set against a backdrop of the crisp lines of the building. Bunting adds a festive, patriotic touch.

Christmas Scene, 39" x 32",
#4- and 6-cut as-is wool on
monk's cloth. Designed and
hooked by Betty Bouchard,
Richmond, Vermont, 1999.

shining down on a manger, surrounded by
farm animals.

Through your rug hooking, you can
create scenes that are autobiographical,
recording observations of the life around
you. Or, you can tell a story, depicting

events real or imaged. Your work may
evoke strong emotions, open to interpretation by each individual viewer.

As you think about the elements that
may inspire your hooked rug landscape,
keep these important points in mind.

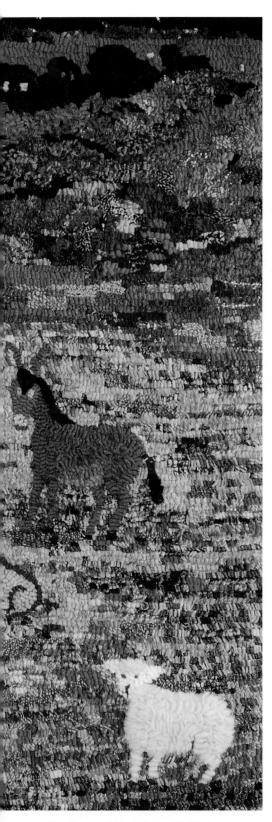

Sky Shapes, 12" x 31", novelty fabrics, yarns, and ribbon on burlap. Designed and hooked by Molly Dye, Jacksonville, Vermont, 2004. McGown trained Molly Dye shows a night scene in a new light with unusual materials.

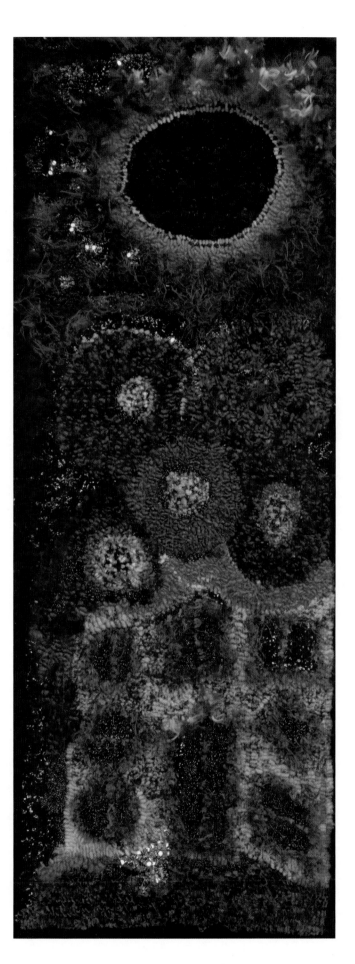

The Dales, 24" x 32", novelty fabrics, yarns, and ribbon on linen. Designed and hooked by Molly Dye, Jacksonville, Vermont, 2005.

Do not be hampered by reality. If you are trying to depict a particular view that actually exists, think carefully about what real elements you want to include in your composition. If you are drawn to a street scene, do you include the parking meters and trash barrels that line the sidewalk? As you gaze at distant mountains, do you want to include the utility poles that cut a swath through the view?

If you wish to hook a rug inspired by a photograph, consider whether the items clearly understandable and identifiable in the original picture will translate well into a hooked rug. I had a student who was hooking an old log cabin that had been in his family for generations. A wood overhang on the side of the cabin was clearly part of the construction when you saw the cabin in a photograph. However, try as he might, he could not make that overhang make sense when it was hooked into the rug. His classmates asked, "What is that?"

If there are elements in your composition that need to be explained to the viewer, think about whether or not you want to include them in your final design. If these elements are important to you, then by all means, create them as you like and don't worry about whether other people understand your work. If you want your viewer to know, without question, precisely what you are trying to depict, then edit out elements that are puzzling or confusing.

Clarity in your artistic interpretation does not mean the landscape you create must be realistic. Your unique vision will help you to interpret a landscape in a way that is entirely your own, regardless of whether or not the viewer sees it the way you do. Your fresh perspective is what makes you an artist. Molly Dye designed and hooked *The Dales* based on her interpretation of the Yorkshire Dales of Northern England. Would I know this rug depicts Yorkshire without the title giving me a clue? Does it matter? To me, it does not, and the artistic integrity of the piece easily stands on its own.

Untitled, 35" x 23", #2-cut as-is and over-dyed wool on burlap. Designer and year unknown. Hooked by Louise Mullen, Dummerston, Vermont. Jen Lavoie's family found this rug after her grandmother, Louise Mullen, passed away. They don't know the year it was hooked, or whether or not Louise was the designer. Jen is restoring the rug because the burlap backing has severely decayed. Note how the bridge is shadowed in the swirling water.

Running Away, 16" x 21", #6-cut hand-dyed wool on linen. Designed and hooked by Diane Kelly, Dorset, Vermont, 2001. Diane replicated a black and white photograph of herself, taken by her grandparents when she was a child. She chose to mimic a sepia effect to soften and age the image. A single dye formula in many values was used for all the wool in this piece.

Have you ever taken a photograph of a spectacular view, only to find the picture never comes close to the magical splendor of seeing the scene in real life? A friend says, "The lens doesn't lie." What does this mean? It is as if the photograph emphasizes reality, while the brain, when seeing the view in real time, edits reality so you only notice the elements to which you are most drawn.

When hooking a scene based on a photograph, how can you decide which elements to include in your final design? Try this simple exercise to help you edit your hooked rug composition.

1. Take a photograph of a view you love. Do not look at the photo just yet.
2. Make a list of what you remember from the view you photographed. Look at the photo only after you complete your list.
3. Start a new list, writing down what you see in the photograph that you do not recall from the moment you shot the picture.

Portrait of Mila, 16" x 21", #3- and 4-cut hand-dyed and as-is wool on burlap. Designed with help from Roslyn Logsdon and based on a black and white 1945 photograph of Joseph Bouchard's mother. Hooked by Betty Bouchard, Richmond, Vermont, 1995. Note how the scattering of little hooked strips of wool in the foreground mimics grass.

4. Add to this list all the elements you see in the photo that you may remember from the initial view, but do not want to include in your final hooked rug design.

Study your lists and use them to help you determine how accurately you want to copy the view in the photograph. I tried this exercise, photographing a beautiful round barn in Vermont's Northeast Kingdom. I recalled the architectural wonder of the barn, and the verdant mountains in the distance.

When I finally looked at the photo, I noticed elements I hadn't even recognized when I pressed the camera's shutter: an ugly, rusted-out pick-up truck, an old crumpled newspaper on the side of the road, and multiple strands of power lines weaving across the sky. These realities of agricultural life were not part of the view I envisioned when I romantically focused on the barn with a backdrop of rolling hills.

The Devil's Workshop,
20" x 18", #4-cut hand-dyed
wool on burlap. Designed
and hooked by Molly Dye,
Jacksonville, Vermont, 1998.
Molly is facile with traditional
and nontraditional techniques
and materials.

As a hooked rug fiber artist, you can experiment by exaggerating the proportion and scale of grand elements of your landscape. Mountains, water, sky, trees, and clouds are ideal objects for this type of treatment. However, keep in mind that if the contrast and scale of detailed elements are wrong, the viewer may become confused. I once hooked a landscape with what I thought were bales of hay. My husband thought they were sunflowers. I didn't want my hay bales to be abstract interpretations, so I re-hooked them three times without success. I eventually gave up and tore them out entirely.

As you look for inspiration for a hooked rug landscape design, ask yourself why you are drawn to a particular scene. What interests you about an image? Are you drawn to the color, scale, subject, or your own emotional response? Do you want to be there, in the scene? Do you want to know more about what you are looking at? Abandon preconceived notions of right and wrong and try to explore your own impulses. Remember you will not create an actual landscape. Rather, you will put together a combination of shapes, colors, and tonal values that, when seen together, give the illusion of a landscape. Most importantly, explore, experiment, and enjoy the path to finding your inspiration.

CHAPTER 3

Composing Your Hooked Rug Landscape

omposition is the act of combining parts or elements to form a whole. Consider theses principles and elements of design to help you compose your hooked rug landscape.

Balance. You may not have the formal training to be able to describe why you believe something is balanced. However, you probably know balance when you see it. Composition is usually thought of in terms of symmetrical, radial, and asymmetrical balance. Symmetrical balance is

Wisteria, 15" x 16", #3- and 4-cut hand-dyed and as-is wool on rug warp. Designed and hooked by Betty Bouchard, Richmond, Vermont, 1998.

Bloomin' Sunflowers, Seeded by Patty, 25" x 29", #4- to 6- cut hand-dyed wool on linen. Designed and hooked by Tony Latham, Montreal, Quebec, 2008. This rug was inspired by the late Patty Yoder who was Tony's friend and mentor. Photo courtesy of Jocelyn Guindon.

a layout of elements, where one side of the composition is like a mirror image of the other. *The Drowning Sea* is symmetrical. The setting sun is in the center of the composition. The ocean, sky, and distant land masses frame the sun equally on the left and right sides of the composition. Betty Bouchard's *Wisteria* is another example of symmetrical balance. The distant house is in the center of the composition. The picket fence and wisteria bushes are positioned almost as though they are mirror images of each other.

Radial balance results when the key element is positioned in the center of a composition, and seems to move outwards on all sides. Tony Latham's *Bloomin' Sunflowers, Seeded by Patty* demonstrates radial balance.

Landscapes depicted in art are most frequently asymmetrical. The composition's focus will often be the largest element, such as a tree, which is positioned off center. The composition is then balanced by either a series of smaller elements on the opposite side of the

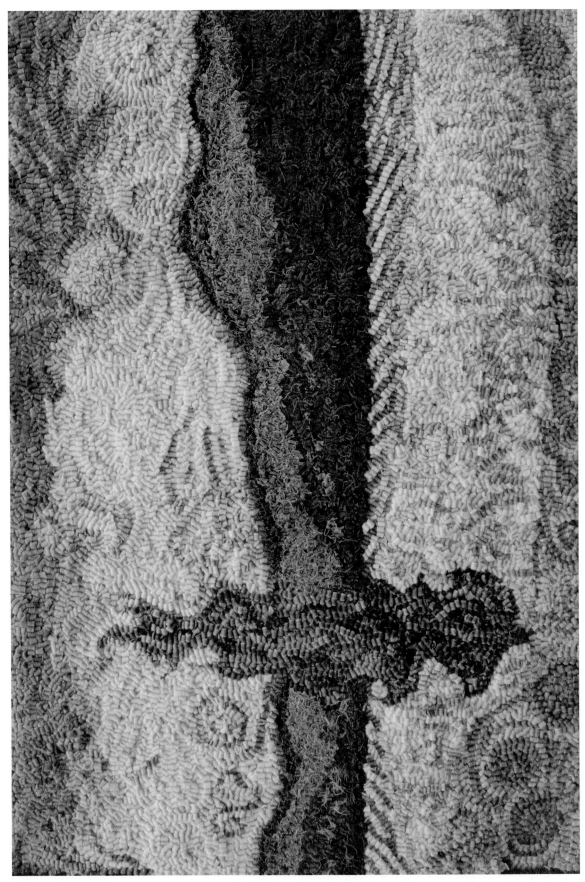

Cedar in Hayfield, 28" x 18", #7-cut over-dyed and hand-dyed wool on monk's cloth. Designed and hooked by Anne-Marie Littenberg, Burlington, Vermont, 2004. This rug represents an example of asymmetrical balance in composition.

Black Is the Color of My True Love's Nose, 26" x 43", #3- to 6-cut recycled and over-dyed wool on linen. Designed and hooked by Jen Lavoie, Huntington, Vermont, 2003. The landscape provides the background for Jen's family's dogs. Dogs who were living at the time this was designed look directly at the viewer.

composition, or a horizontal element that stretches for a length at least as wide as the main element is high. *Cedar in Hayfield* is a simple example of asymmetrical balance. The cedar tree on the left is in the foreground. It is balanced by the mountain range that spreads across the far distance. Note the mountains on the right are taller than those behind the cedar tree. This difference in height creates a sense of balance in the piece, even though there is, strictly speaking, no symmetry.

Black is the Color of My True Love's Nose depicts a very large white dog on the right. He takes up the greatest amount of space of any single element in the composition. He is balanced, however, by the smaller, red-collared black dog on the left. The large size of one light element can be balanced by the deep intensity of value (the black dog) or color of a smaller element (the dog's red collar). The horizontal flow of the landscape background reinforces the balance.

Harmony and unity. How do your design elements relate to what you are trying to express? Do you have a combination of related elements that make sense to the viewer? Is your design visually pleasing? My father tells me *Wine Dark Sea* doesn't work for him because he is unable to understand what he is supposed to be looking at. I explained I was trying to get the effect of sunset at a time of day when you cannot tell where the ocean ends and the sky begins. My composition is too abstract and confusing for my father's taste.

Wine Dark Sea, 14" x 14", #4-cut hand-painted wool on monk's cloth. Designed and hooked by Anne-Marie Littenberg, Burlington, Vermont, 2007. An abstract sunset over water, this piece confuses some viewers.

Hinesburg, Vermont,
32" x 25", #6- and 8-cut
over-dyed and as-is wool on
monk's cloth. Designed and
hooked by Rae Harrell,
Hinesburg, Vermont, 2002;
from the collection of
Ramsey Yoder.

Once you have decided on the subject for your hooked rug landscape,
you must consider the overall proportion of the finished piece. Should it be
square, horizontal, vertical, or some
other shape? If it's going to be a rectangle, what ratio of height to width
should you use?

We often automatically choose to
work in a rectangular shape that mimics the approximate proportions of a
3 x 5 index card. I don't know what the
source of this cultural bias is; perhaps it
is the fact that as children we were
given drawing paper that was similarly
proportioned. As rug hookers, sometimes our biases may be based on the

proportions generally used for floor
mats and carpets. In creating a hooked
rug landscape, you want to consider
whether automatically defaulting to a
familiar shape or size is the best way to
realize your vision as an artist. The following exercise will help you chose a
shape that enhances the artistic interest
and integrity of your work.

1. Take six pieces of 8¹/₂" x 11"
paper. On the first piece, draw a square
that is 8" long on each side. Position
your second sheet horizontally, and
draw a rectangle that is 8" high by 10"
wide. Position your third sheet of paper
vertically, and draw a rectangle that is
10" high by 8" wide. Position your

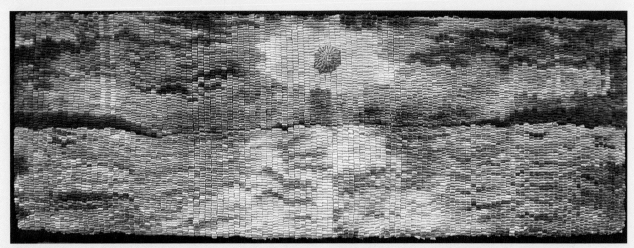

The Drowning Sea, 34" x 13", #7-cut hand-painted wool on monk's cloth. Designed and hooked by Anne-Marie Littenberg, Burlington, Vermont, 2007. This exemplifies formal balance, where the left and right sides of the composition are mirror images of each other.

fourth piece of paper horizontally. Draw a rectangle that is 4" high by 10" wide. Position your fifth piece of paper vertically and draw a rectangle that is 10" high by 4" wide. On your sixth (and last) sheet of paper, draw the largest free-form outline you can fit on the paper (perhaps kidney-bean shaped). You now have six differently shaped and proportioned backgrounds to use for sketching a landscape.

2. Think of three simple elements you might include in a landscape; for instance, a moon, a little house, and a tree. Draw a landscape depicting these three elements on each of the six differently shaped and proportioned backgrounds.

What have you learned in your efforts to position these identical elements on six differently shaped backgrounds? Does the proportion and shape of one background in particular best suit the composition of your landscape? Which background is the easiest to work with? Which is the hardest? Which gives you the most pleasing effect? Did you change the size or scale of the elements to make them work on the different backgrounds?

Once in a Blue Moon, 19" x 41", novelty fabrics, yarns, and ribbon on burlap. Designed and hooked by Molly Dye, Jacksonville, Vermont, 2005. How would the effect of this composition change if Molly had hooked it on a differently shaped backing?

The Home Farm
(triptych), three
15" x 30" panels,
#3- to 8-cut hand-dyed,
over-dyed, and recycled
wool, plus mohair, silk
and possum yarns, and
dyed fleece on linen.
Designed and hooked
by Carolyn Buttolph, St.
Johnsbury, Vermont,
2007. Inspired by
Carolyn's family farm in
Shoreham, Vermont.
According to Carolyn,
"By making a triptych,
each element (the
house, barns, truck, man,
dog, trees) is allowed to
have a larger presence
within its panel than it
would if it were just part
of a single rug. Also,
interest is added by the
tension set up between
the panels and how
they relate to each
other." Photos courtesy
of George Bouret.

Charlton Idyll, 60" x 36", hand-cut over-dyed wool on burlap. Designed and hooked by Jule Marie Smith, Ballston Spa, New York, 1983.

When someone looks at your design, can they discern what you are trying to depict? Is it important to you that your composition be understandable? I had a student working on a western landscape. She wanted to depict horizontal striations of rock formations in the desert. Her horizontal lines were so perfectly straight and positioned that they looked like telephone lines without the utility poles. She was adamant that her interpretation was accurate, and adhering to her vision was far more important than creating an element other viewers could easily understand.

As a rug hooking artist, you must make a critical decision in designing your landscape: If you have to explain your design elements to the viewer, does the composition work artistically? Or, is it important to you for a personal reason to include otherwise confusing elements? Someone once explained to me that a member of her family would be insulted if her finished piece omitted an element I found puzzling. The rug designer chose to please her family rather than focus on the artistic cohesion of her work. As the creator of your hooked rug, it is up to you to balance personal priorities in making your ultimate choices.

Once you have designed your individual elements, how do you put them together to compose the entire scene? Do the style, color, scale, positioning, and shapes of your elements make sense within your rug? Compare Jule Marie Smith's *Charlton Idyll* with Molly Dye's *Many Moons*. Both depict a town or village from a distance. Both have architecturally distinct buildings under the umbrella of broad skies. Yet, the two rugs are vastly different. The style, shape, and colors of Molly's buildings and spires make sense within the context of Molly's rug. How would the piece look if the yellow house from *Charlton Idyll* was transplanted to *Many Moons*? The combination would be bizarre, lacking harmony and unity. Within the context of each individual rug,

Many Moons, 30" x 24", novelty fabrics, yarns, and ribbon on linen. Designed and hooked by Molly Dye, Jacksonville, Vermont, 2005. Molly created this piece in memory of Patty Yoder.

Stressa, Lake Maggiore Region, 40" x 24", novelty fabrics, yarns, and ribbon on linen. Designed and hooked by Molly Dye, Jacksonsville, Vermont, 2006. Molly's view of this mountainous landscape in Italy.

The Thaw, 52" x 27", wool yarn on cotton rug warp. Designed and hooked by Anne-Marie Littenberg, Burlington, Vermont, 1999. I was inspired by raging rivers that burst through the snow and ice when spring finally arrives in northern Vermont.

however, the buildings, color schemes, and layout make sense. How would a patterned border work for Molly's rug? Her design elements are numerous, quite strong, and distinct, forming a busy composition. The rug is visually exciting, and the addition of a complex border would give the eye no place to rest. Jule's composition, however, works beautifully with the rolling shapes of her border, which mimic the rolling hills and soft colors of her bucolic town. Her sky provides a broad expanse for visual rest. Molly's sky explodes with the night. Each work is beautiful and intriguing in its own way.

I have had the privilege of watching both Jule and Molly design their rugs. While many hooked rug fiber artists have their designs established well before the hooking begins, these ladies each work more spontaneously, designing as they go along. The placement of elements, color choices, scale, and patterning of their rugs emerges as the work progresses. The fin-

Our Vermont Woods in Early Autumn, 26" x 21", #6-cut hand-dyed wool on linen. Designed and hooked by Diane Kelly, Dorset, Vermont, 2007. Diane writes, "I looked out the window on a late September morning and there was a spot in the woods that the streamers of morning sunlight had set ablaze."

ished product is as much of a surprise to them as it is to the viewer. Their designs are also very thoughtful. They do not hesitate to pull out and re-design (and of course, re-hook) any areas of their rugs that are not ultimately satisfying.

Rhythm and movement. When someone looks at your piece, how does his or her eye move through the composition? Does the eye move in quick, abrupt jumps, or slowly and smoothly? Hard, jagged edges and hot colors can force the eye to move in a way that is exciting and unexpected. Cool colors and flowing lines move the viewer's eye in a gentler rhythm. Molly Dye's *Stressa, Lake Maggiore Region* excites the eye with hot

pinks and oranges, and angular, jutting shapes. My eye first travels to the raspberry colored diamond in the middle of the furthest, center mountain peak. It then travels along the jagged mountain range, and finally up to the swirling, wild sky. My eye moves sharply, in an upward motion. With my rug, *The Thaw,* the eye first lights on the upper right corner, and then flows down directly to the lower left.

When viewing *Our Vermont Woods in Early Autumn* by Diane Kelly, my eye is first drawn to the warm light coming from the upper right and through the center of the stand of trees. My eye follows the light down and to the left, to the base of the birch trees. Then, the gentle

Shadows, 30" x 31", #6- to 8-cut over-dyed and as-is wool on rug warp. Designed and hooked by Mary Lee O'Connor, Ballston Spa, New York, 2007.

Beyond the Garden Gate, 26" x 22", various plied threads of linen, silk, cotton, polyester, wool, etc. on rug warp. Designed and hooked by Anne-Marie Littenberg, Burlington, Vermont, 2005. It doesn't make sense that the sun is shining underneath the tree, especially since the sky is swirling with storm clouds. I should have included shadows.

slope of the green foreground moves my eye across the bottom of the rug to the right, where it finally lands in the thick of the evergreens. I can almost feel my pulse quicken when I see Molly's rug. With Diane's, I get the sense I could take a nap in the quiet, glowing woods. My reactions to each are vastly different but equally positive.

Choosing hard, jagged lines or flowing, circular lines can influence how the viewer's eye moves among the elements of a hooked rug landscape. In addition, the use of gradations of value helps to move the eye. Your eye is first drawn to saturated bright and dark value elements of a rug. At this point a juxtaposition of contrasting elements (something dark

Blue Heron at Sunset on Lake Minnetonka, 34" x 25", #6- and 8-cut wool on linen. Designed and hooked by Lucinda Pratt, Excelsior, Minnesota, 2007. Photo courtesy of Lucinda Pratt.

Wherever you roam

1763 1912

Wherever you wander

Be happy Be healthy

And glad to be home

Glad to Be Home, 47" x 47", #-3, 6-, and 8-cut as-is and hand-dyed wool on linen. Designed and hooked by Gail Duclos Lapierre, Shelburne, Vermont, 2001. This portrait of Gail's dairy farm was completed weeks before tragedy struck and the barn was burned to the ground. The silo still stands.

against a light back ground, or sharply shaped and defined against a duller, flowing background) often occurs. Your eye then moves on to lighter, dulled-down, or grey colors and values. The movement of the viewer's eye is also influenced by repetition of pattern and shapes. Note in *Shadows* by Mary Lee O'Connor, the shape and pattern of tree branches is repeated in the ground shadows.

Emphasis. What is the dominant element in your composition? The dominant element is the item with the most visual weight. It is often found in the

foreground of a piece. Secondary emphasis usually goes to something in the midground. Subordinate elements often recede into the distance. In *Beyond the Garden Gate,* the dominant element is the maple tree blazing with fall colors in the right foreground. Its color is hot, and it contrasts starkly with the yellow grass and duller mountains in the distance. The mountains are of secondary emphasis. Figures in the foreground provide bold focus when viewed from a distance. Subsidiary scenes and decorative details are seen upon closer inspection.

NORTH ROAD FARM

When designing your rug, limit the number of elements to which you plan to give strong emphasis. Too much pattern and detail can make it difficult for the viewer to understand what you are trying to depict. Of course, some rug hookers are masterful in their ability to successfully combine many strong elements, and you may be one of them. But if you are creating your first hooked rug landscape, I urge you to keep it simple.

Proportion. Proportion is the relationship between one element and another. Does the scale of each element make sense in the context of the rest of the composition? The proportion of one element to another does not have to be realistic because this is art. But if you choose to exaggerate proportion, do so in a way that does not confuse the viewer. Cindy

Pratt exaggerates the proportion of her bird in *Blue Heron at Sunset on Lake Minnetonka*. Although proportion is exaggerated, the viewer is able to discern that one element, the largest, is a blue heron, even though in reality the bird would never be larger than the dock.

Exaggerated proportion works very well with primitive hooking. Gail Duclos Lapierre exaggerated the scale of her dairy cows in the upper right of *Glad to Be Home*. Note the size and position of the cows in relation to the barn, and you realize they would be enormous beasts if this rug represented realistic proportions. The size of the car and figures in Diane Kelly's *North Road Farm* is not exaggerated. It seems realistic in relation to the size and positioning of the house and surrounding foliage.

North Road Farm, 25" x 20", #6-cut over-dyed and as-is wool on linen. Pattern was drawn by Roslyn Logsdon based on a photograph. Hooked by Diane Kelly, Dorset, Vermont, 2002.

Fall Line, 44" x 28", #4-cut hand-dyed wool on burlap. Designed and hooked by Molly Dye, Jacksonville, Vermont, 2001.

The phrase I hear most frequently from students designing their hooked rug landscape is "I can't draw." The good news is you don't need to be good at drawing. Instead, you can use a number of tools to compliment the princi- ples and elements of design when composing your hooked rug land- scape: a camera, tracing paper, a sketchbook, colored pencils and crayons, the library, a computer, and photocopying services.

Hadley III, 17" x 14", #4-cut hand-dyed wool on burlap. Designed and hooked by Molly Dye, Jacksonville, Vermont, 2003.

Untitled, 9" x 11", fine-cut wool on burlap. Unknown designer, hooker, and year. Diane Kelly's parents bought this mat on a ski trip to Quebec in the 1950s.

Untitled, 8" x 11", fine-cut wool on burlap. Unknown designer, hooker, and year. Diane Kelly's parents bought this mat on a ski trip to Quebec in the 1950s.

The digital camera is an invaluable tool. I keep a small one in my purse so it is always available if I see a view I might want to use in a future hooked rug landscape. It's also a great resource for collecting images of trees, moun-

tains, and other elements you may wish to copy and add to your composition. If you wish to design a rug based on a specific view, photograph that view over the course of time. Photograph the same view during different

Four AM Milking, 28" x 20", #6-cut hand-dyed and over-dyed wool on linen. Designed and hooked by Diane Kelly, Dorset, Vermont, 2007. Diane Kelly's memories of a drive from New York City to a ski weekend in Vermont from thirty years ago inspired this rug. It provides an interesting pastoral contrast with hooked mats depicting mid-century winter scenes from Quebec.

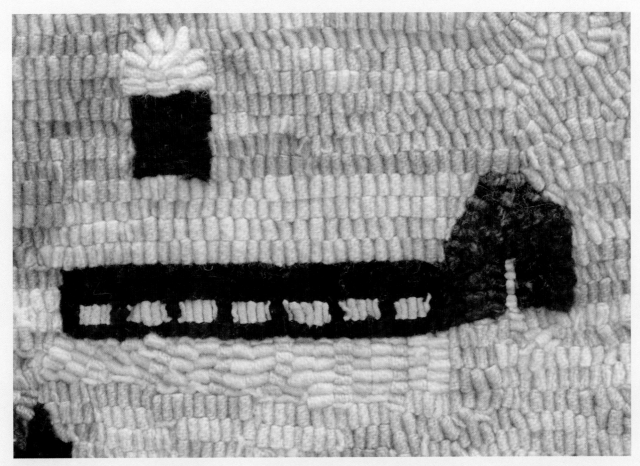

hours of the day, at various times of year, and under changing weather conditions. How does the light change from morning to night? How does the foliage evolve as the seasons pass?

A sketchpad and tracing paper have so many applications. If you have no confidence in your drawing ability, practice by repeatedly tracing elements you admire from books, photos, magazines, and other publications. Use colored pencils and crayons to experiment with color. The practice of repeatedly tracing elements will help teach you how to sketch them. Keep in mind that you are doing this solely for the purpose of practicing your sketching and drawing abilities. Do not trace other people's copyrighted work from photos and books and use them without appropriate permission in your hooked rugs. Copyright laws protect an artist's work for the life of the artist plus 70 years. Thus, if you want to trace and copy an element from a 200-year-old painting, it is legal in most

cases. But if you trace and copy elements of the work of an artist who has died within the last 70 years, you are breaking the law if you use those elements without permission of the artist or whoever owns the copyright to his work.

Repeatedly tracing so you get the gist of how to draw something is perfectly legitimate. In fact, copying pictures in art museums for educational purposes has been a cornerstone of classical art training for centuries. The more you practice by tracing and copying, the more adept and confident you will become when the time comes to finally design your own original elements and composition.

You may trace elements from pictures that are in the public domain and use them in your hooked rugs. Use a search engine on your computer to look for public domain pictures of any subject you can dream up. In addition, bookstores and libraries often have books of public domain images. Take

Four AM Milking (detail). Diane recalls passing a dairy farm before dawn, when cows were getting their first milking of the day. Barn light glowed on the snow.

P Town, 27" x 19", novelty fabrics, yarns, and ribbon on linen. Designed and hooked by Molly Dye, Jacksonville, Vermont, 2007. Molly Dye's interpretation of a view of Provincetown, Cape Cod.

advantage of the fact that it is fine to trace and copy anything you like, even copyright protected work, for the exclusive purpose of practicing how to draw.

Photocopying services can be an enormously helpful tool. Use a photocopying machine or the service at a local office supply store to shrink and enlarge elements you are playing with in your design. I often shrink and enlarge images from my camera. I get multiple copies made and then cut out the elements in various sizes to see what works with the composition of my design. Sketch a basic cartoon of your planned layout. Take your cutout elements and move them around on the cartoon to help you get a sense of how and where they should be placed in your composition.

The art section of your library or a virtual visit to an art museum (via the Internet) provides an excellent oppor-

tunity for studying landscape art. When I am stumped by choices I have to make in composition, design, color, and so on, I often browse books of landscapes by other artists at my local library. In this way, Vincent van Gogh taught me that it is okay to make my suns purple or green rather than plain old yellow. How did a seventeenth century Dutch landscape painter interpret his countryside? I can visit the Rijksmuseum in Amsterdam through the Internet and see. Use any Internet search engine and type in the name of an artist, or art museum, and you will come to an astonishing array of images you can study for free. The major museums of the world provide access to their collections through the Internet, and their websites often give you the option of visiting in English or in the native language of the host country.

CHAPTER 4

Perspective: Achieving a Sense of Depth

DEPTH AND SCALE

Stephanie Ashworth Krauss' rug, *663 Elm Street*, provides an excellent lesson in the many elements that help achieve a sense of depth and scale in a hooked rug landscape. The position of the receding driveway moves the viewer's eye from the foreground into the carport. Note that the driveway under the carport is shaded. Also note that the bush to the left of the front door casts a subtle shade on the side of the house. Camelshump, one of Vermont's beloved Green Mountains, provides the backdrop frame in the distance. Tiny, to-scale details, such as the mailbox fringed with foliage at the base of the driveway and the little bird to the left of the front lawn, provide additional visual cues about the size of various elements. A clothesline carousel is visible beyond the overhang of the carport.

663 Elm Street, 38" x 28", #4-, 6-, and 8-cut as-is and over-dyed wool on rug warp. Designed and hooked by Stephanie Ashworth Krauss, Montpelier, Vermont, 2008; from the collection of Les Matkowski.

663 Elm Street (details).

As you look at a picture of a landscape, objects that are supposed to appear far away are depicted as smaller and closer together than objects that are nearby, or in the foreground. This technique is used by artists to depict perspective. In real life, the outdoors is three-dimensional. In landscapes depicted in hooked rugs, paintings, or photos, you see a two-dimensional representation of three-dimensional elements.

How do you manipulate elements in your hooked rug landscape when you want to make them appear to be in the distance as opposed to up close? You may study theories of perspective in detail by going to the library or by using a search engine on the Internet and typing in phrases such as "one point perspective,"

"two point perspective," and "three point perspective." You will come across line drawings, exercises, and technical explanations used by artists, architects, and engineers. Here is how some contemporary hooked rug fiber artists have used design elements to achieve a sense of depth in their hooked rug landscapes.

Polly Alexander's *Laundry Day* clearly demonstrates some simple ways to achieve perspective. It provides an excellent lesson in the positioning and enhancement of items in the foreground, mid-ground, and background. First, look at the laundry line that stretches from the distant white house on the left to the immediate right foreground. The clothes in the foreground have the most space between them. The clothes seem to get closer together the far-

Corn (detail), #3- to 6-cut as-is, over-dyed, and hand-painted wool on linen. Designed and hooked by Jen Lavoie, Huntington, Vermont, 2007. A distant red barn is framed by stalks of corn. Note that the directional hooking and variations of value make the individual leaves distinct. They contrast with the flat hooking of the sky. The ground appears duller as it recedes toward the barn. (See full rug on page 53.)

Laundry Day, 44" x 28",
#4- to 6-cut over-dyed and
as-is wool on linen,
embellished with chenille,
nylon, wool appliqué,
buttons, and ribbon. Designed
and hooked by Polly
Alexander, Essex Junction,
Vermont, 2003.

ther away they are on the line. In addition, note the size of the clothes. The bikini and blue plaid dress each measure much larger than the size of the distant house. Objects closer to the house are proportionally smaller. The laundry on this line provides an excellent example of how to place items in a way that conveys depth in a scene. You get a real sense of things being nearby, farther away, and in the distance.

Look carefully at the rug, and you will see that about one-third of it is comprised of a mid-value shade of green, which is flatly hooked wool. This green is used to portray a distant rolling hill, or mountain, and also the lawn around the white house. How did Polly use this simple hooking, with no shading, to convey the image of a mid-ground lawn and distant mountains, all out of the same flat wool? Note the simple vertical lines of brown that seem to run in back of the white house. This picket fence image delineates the mid- from the far-ground and fools the viewer's eye into perceiving the same flat color block of green as both nearby lawn and distant mountain.

Adding a fence to a landscape composition is a neat trick for conveying a sense of depth. In *Waiting,* a fence begins in the center foreground of the composition and moves off into the distance before making a left turn to enclose a field. Note the positioning and size of the fence rails. Up close, they are large. The rails become smaller and closer together in the distance.

Perspective achieves a sense of depth and the impression that elements are three-dimensional. Shading and shadows are an effective way to accomplish this. If you wish to add shadows, first figure out the source of the light in your composition. In *Waiting,* the color of the sky tells us the light comes from the left. The right edge of the fence posts and the right side of the cottonwood trunk are shaded with darker values. I also added a shadow under the tree, which helps to anchor it in the composition.

A road that rolls from the foreground to a distant vanishing point is another effective element for conveying a sense of depth in a composition. The road in *Waiting* begins in the lower right of the rug and disappears to a vanishing point somewhere close to the center of the design. If you wish to include other elements in the

Waiting, 31" x 24", various plied threads of linen, silk, cotton, polyester, wool, etc. on rug warp. Designed and hooked by Anne-Marie Littenberg, Burlington, Vermont, 2007.

The Woman on the Swing
(detail), #4- and 5-cut as-is
and over-dyed wool on linen.
Designed and hooked by Jen
Lavoie, Huntington, Vermont,
2003. Directional hooking and
a graying of values enhance
the sense of this baled hay
field receding into the
distance. (See full rug on
page 63.)

composition, play with their position so their size and shape are appropriate to where they are placed in relation to the receding road. The size of the cottonwood tree on the right makes sense for its position in relation to the road. Moving the same-sized tree closer to the foreground or farther into the distance would have created an odd proportion. The tree would have looked wrong.

Elements such as roads, fences, and shadows contribute to the illusion of depth. Color and value do, too. Warm colors and dark values enhance a sense of something being up close. Cool and dulled-down colors and lighter values impart a sense of something receding. Polly Alexander's *My Mountain Men* demonstrates this with the warm oranges of the foliage in the foreground of her composition. Her mountains become lighter and more dull or gray as they recede.

My Mountain Men, 32" x 22", #4-, 5-, and 6-cut over-dyed and as-is wool on linen. Designed and hooked by Polly Alexander, Essex Junction, Vermont, 2000.

CHAPTER 5

Contrast: The "Worker Bee" of Composition

Contrast provides emphasis, and allows the viewer's brain to distinguish shapes. What does this mean? Look at a black and white photograph of your favorite scene. Even though it is devoid of color, you are able to tell what is a mountain, building, road, or tree. You can distinguish the various elements because of texture, tonal value, and transition, even though the image provides no clues through color.

Contrast created through texture is achieved with directional hooking and material choices. It is especially effective for up-close viewing of your work. Textural contrast can be achieved by incorporating different cuts and weaves of wool, utilizing various dye effects, and employing nontraditional materials and embellishments. Jocelyn Guindon's use of texture in *Soleil Levant sur Harbor Point* shows how roving can give the impression of lupine and how the patterning of hooked loops (through a basket weave stitch)

Soleil Levant sur Harbor Point, 37" x 24³/₄", #4- and 6-cut wool plus roving on monk's cloth. Designed and hooked by Jocelyn Guindon, Montreal, Quebec, 2005. Photo courtesy of Jocelyn Guindon.

Soleil Levant sur Harbor Point (detail). A basket stitch adds texture, giving the suggestion that the cottage is sided with cedar shingles. Texture and directional hooking allow the artist to distinguish between the cottage and the tree stump, even though they are hooked with the same wool selections. Photo courtesy of Jocelyn Guindon.

Little White Church, 16" round, #3- and 4-cut as-is and hand-dyed wool on burlap. Designed by Joan Moshimer. Hooked by Betty Bouchard, Richmond, Vermont, 1999. Different values and color tones of off-white, combined with directional hooking, help the viewer see contrast between the church and snow.

A Walk #3 (detail), #3- to 6-cut recycled and over-dyed wool on linen. Designed and hooked by Jen Lavoie, Huntington, Vermont, 2005. Many values and textures of similar colors, combined with directional hooking, can be used in a way that allows the viewer to see tree trunks, bark, a shaded path, and the figures' trousers. (See full rug on page 52.)

can mimic cedar shingles on a cottage. Directional hooking helps the eye distinguish window frames. Note that while the color and value of the tree stump are similar to that of the cottage, the viewer can distinguish these as separate elements because of directional hooking.

Tonal value, or the sense that something is light, medium, or dark, is another way of achieving contrast, and it is highly effective when combined with directional hooking. Note how Betty Bouchard uses generous quantities of off-white wool in different values and color tones in *Little*

The Girl on a Rock (detail), #3- to 6-cut recycled and over-dyed wool on linen. Designed and hooked by Jen Lavoie, Huntington, Vermont, 2003. (See full rug on page 5.)

White Church. The direction of her hooking, and combination of off-whites subtly tinged with pinks, greens, blues, and grays, helps the viewer distinguish the church from snow on the ground and snow draping the evergreen trees. The church's lines are crisp and straight. The snow on the ground swirls in flowing waves. Snow in the trees clings to ruffled boughs. The detail photo of Jen Lavoie's *A Walk* demonstrates how multiple values and textures of a limited number of colors (here, browns and grays) can be used with directional hooking to help the viewer see the whorls and ridges of tree bark distinct from the shadows that cross a walking path.

Transition plays a key role in contrast. Transition refers to how individual elements are edged, a motif is framed, or the viewer's eye moves from one part of a composition to another. The detail photo from *The Girl on a Rock* shows toy trucks. You can distinguish the white truck on the right from the surrounding rocks because of its angular shape. Also, lines of dark wool are used to outline the parts of the truck that border on rocks. Note the

entire cab of the white truck is not completely outlined with dark wool. Rocks are distinguished from each other by their individual shapes and the judicious use of light and dark partial outlines. Individual rocks are not each completely outlined by single strips of wool. Rather, bits and pieces of light and dark wool are used only in places where the value of the body of an individual rock is similar to the value of its neighbor. Also note the subtle transition between soil positioned just beyond the rocks, and the start of foliage farther back. The viewer isn't quite certain where the soil ends and the foliage begins. The juxtaposition of sharp and subtle transition adds to the interest of the composition. It also mimics reality. When you look at a view, there are elements you can clearly identify separately (a tree from a barn, for instance). Others may be more difficult to distinguish (where does a field end and the distant mountains begin?).

Transition plays a key role in understanding details in Jen Lavoie's *Canyon de Chelly.* The light value and rounded shape of the cottonwood leaves help the viewer

Canyon de Chelly, 39" x 60", #3- to 5-cut as-is, recycled, and hand-painted wool on linen. Designed and hooked by Jen Lavoie, Huntington, Vermont, 2007.

tell them apart from the canyon walls, which are of darker value and hooked in a sharp, more angular shape. Note that the canyon walls are hooked vertically. Their transition is distinct against the blue, horizontal hooking of the sky.

In *Let's Play in the Moonlight,* I used bright yellow and lavender to outline the evergreen trees. Without the outline, the transition from trees to night sky would have been too subtle and the trees would have been difficult to distinguish. The transition from the ground under the trees to the ground under the figures of the person and dog is more gradual. No bold, clear lines delineate one part of the ground from another.

Let's Play in the Moonlight (detail), various plied threads of linen, silk, cotton, polyester, wool, etc. on verel. Designed and hooked by Anne-Marie Littenberg, Burlington, Vermont, 2005; from the collection of Sharon Townsend. Trees were outlined in light values so they would stand out from the night sky. This crisp transition between tree and sky contrasts with the gradual transition between the ground under the trees and that under the figure and dog. (See full rug on page 4.)

I have provided you with transition examples that employ very little outline and fill. We rug hookers often use the outline and fill method in our compositions, and I would encourage you to try more subtle ways of transitioning between elements. Outline and fill is effective in primitives and many other applications. But it can also lend a cartoonlike quality to your rug. See if you can create a composition where you do not automatically uniformly outline each element in dark wool and then fill in the blank space within the outline. This practice may help you achieve a more painterly quality to your work.

A Walk (triptych), three 36" x 32" panels, #3- to 6-cut recycled and over-dyed wool on linen. Designed and hooked by Jen Lavoie, Huntington, Vermont, 2006.

What is the perspective of the viewer when he or she looks at a hooked rug landscape? We tend to design our rugs so the viewer seems to be standing in the same position one would while photographing a scene or watching a movie. Our perspective is often that of a person, slightly removed but on ground level, gazing out at something in the distance. How can we change our viewpoint to add interest and mystery to our work?

Jen Lavoie creates hooked rug landscapes with unique perspectives. In the first panel of *A Walk,* the viewer is positioned as a small woodland creature peering over a fern from a gentle rise above the two figures. You see the scene from the point of view of a tiny, distant observer, intently watching someone else's intimate moment. How often do we get down to the level of ground foliage to look out at a scene? It is a highly unusual perspective. *Corn* shows the view of a far-off red barn, fully framed by gorgeous stalks of silk-tasseled corn. It is as if the cornrow is a telescope, zeroing in on the structure.

The Woman in the Red Wool Suit provides the most interesting and unusual perspective in any rug I've ever seen about landscapes. It

incorporates numerous unexpected points of view. The composition itself is not a landscape. It is a view of the inside of an art museum. The landscape elements are introduced through the paintings displayed on the gallery walls. You can easily identify Jen's interpretations (not copies!) of specific works by Canadian Masters such as Frank Johnston (*Looking into the Sky,* 1919, partially viewed on the left), Lawren Harris (*Red House, Winter,* 1925, center right), and Tom Thomson (*Autumn Foliage,* 1916, center left).

If you look at the perspective of this rug, you realize the observer is looking down, from a substantial height, at the elegant woman in red. The observer would literally have to be a fly on a wall to view the scene as depicted in Jen's rug. This piece was inspired by a moment Jen experienced in the National Gallery of Canada in Ottawa, Ontario. She was struck by the large chamber empty of everything except glorious landscape paintings and a solitary, glamorous lady of a certain age who seemed mesmerized by art. The lady was magnificently dressed and coifed, with perfectly straight seams running down the backs of her stockings.

The artists referenced in Jen's work were known as the Group of Seven. They were twentieth century painters who worked to create art that reflected a unique Canadian sensibility. They did not want to be hampered by the traditions and styles of old Europe that so dominated the art scene of their country at that time. Like the Group of Seven, Jen works to create her own unique vision through her art. She is concerned with expressing her sensibility and style. She is not hampered by the need to capture an exact, historically accurate copy of the moment. For instance, she experimented with different colors in choosing which wool to use for the gallery walls. It wasn't important that she reproduce the actual color of the gallery. Rather, she wanted a color that best complimented her elegant lady, while also enhancing the view of her interpretation of specific paintings by members of the Group of Seven.

What unique viewpoint can you employ in the creation of your next hooked rug landscape?

Corn, 33" x 62", #3- to 6-cut as-is, over-dyed, and hand-painted wool on linen. Designed and hooked by Jen Lavoie, Huntington, Vermont, 2007. From the collection of Sharon Townsend.

The Woman in the Red Wool Suit, 63" x 38", #3- to 6-cut recycled and over-dyed wool on linen.
Designed and hooked by Jen Lavoie, Huntington, Vermont, 2004.

CHAPTER 6

Color

While contrast helps the brain understand what you are looking at, color gives it emotional resonance. Rug hookers are frequently intimidated by color, and many find this aspect of hooked rug design to be the most challenging. Some worry whether their color choices follow established rules of color theory. Concern may center on determining if the finished rug will be appropriate to a decorating scheme or if choices accurately reproduce hues found in nature. Students' lack of confidence in color choice means rug hooking teachers spend an enormous amount of time helping with color planning. I have the sense

more students are concerned about following prescribed notions of the so-called right and wrong usage of color than they are in exploring their own color preferences and instincts or in successfully manipulating other elements of design.

Some rug hookers have a knack for putting together color. But we all see the world with different eyes, and what appears so obviously right to one person, may be profoundly wrong to another. And then there are those who are paralyzed by the thought of having to choose their own colors. They would rather abandon a project than be faced with this seemingly insurmountable task.

The Old Farmhouse, 43" x 28", #4-cut hand-dyed and as-is wool on burlap. Adapted from a Karl Kraft pattern. Hooked by Betty Bouchard, Richmond, Vermont, 1993.

Corn (detail), #3- to 6-cut as-is, over-dyed, and hand-painted wool on linen. Designed and hooked by Jen Lavoie, Huntington, Vermont, 2007; from the collection of Sharon Townsend. The warm red of the corn silk makes it visually pop amidst the swaths of green foliage. (See full rug on page 53.)

Purple Woods, 36" x 24", #6-cut hand-dyed wool on linen. Designed and hooked by Diane Kelly, Dorset, Vermont, 2007. Influenced by Diane's admiration for the artist, Wolf Kahn, she worked in his strong, clear palette.

Valley of North Conway, 22" x 19", #3- and 4-cut as-is and hand-dyed wool on verel. Designed by Jacquelin Hansen. Hooked by Betty Bouchard, Richmond, Vermont, 2000.

Color has an emotional resonance unmatched by other considerations of design. It can influence how we feel, even if we are unconscious of its effect. This is why realtors encourage homeowners to paint their homes in neutral shades (mostly off-white) when trying to sell a house. Making a house color-neutral means it has the least chance of offending anyone with a strong color sensibility. When looking at neutral colors, it is easier for people to envision how they might change the scheme to suit their own taste. Vibrant, hot colors, which one person might find exciting, can be profoundly off-putting to someone else. I love green and purple, while my husband is nauseated by these color choices. (No green is too bilious or acidy for me.)

Color preferences, and notions of its right and wrong use, evolve over time and vary among cultures. One of the old rules of rug hooking is to never use white

Sun Valley, 17" x 17", novelty fabrics, yarns, and ribbon on linen. Designed and hooked by Molly Dye, Jacksonville, Vermont, 2006.

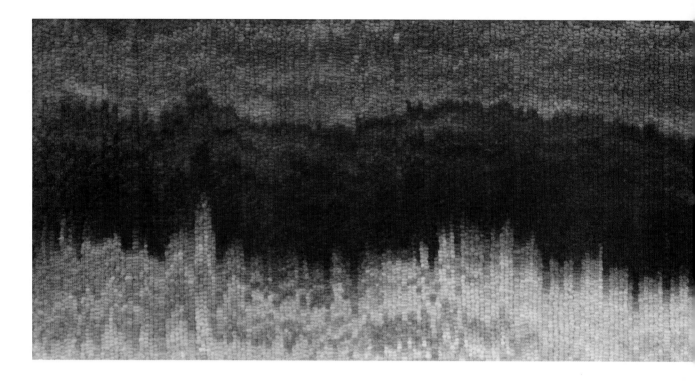

in a design. In recent years, however, I am seeing more white (especially when paired with black) in hooked rugs, and it can be quite effective. Perceptions about the appropriate use of color have strong cultural biases. In North America, black is the traditional color of mourning, while in China white serves that role.

Would a painter heed a critic's caution if told to never use a particular color? Changes in the chemical technology of oil paint and pigments allowed

Blue Barn, Color Study, 24" x 24", #6-cut hand-dyed wool on linen. Designed and hooked by Diane Kelly, Dorset, Vermont, 2008. This is a study of color complements.

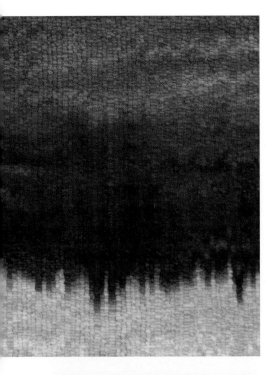

Autumn Splendor, 31" x 11", #3-cut hand-painted wool on monk's cloth. Designed and hooked by Barbara Held, Tinmouth, Vermont, 2007. Barbara is fearless in her use of color. She mixed intense dye solutions of rhodamine red, flavine yellow, and turquoise, adding a touch of black for some of the blue and purple in the sky. She was generous with her use of citric acid to hold her colors and keep them from bleeding as she hand-painted the dye onto her wool.

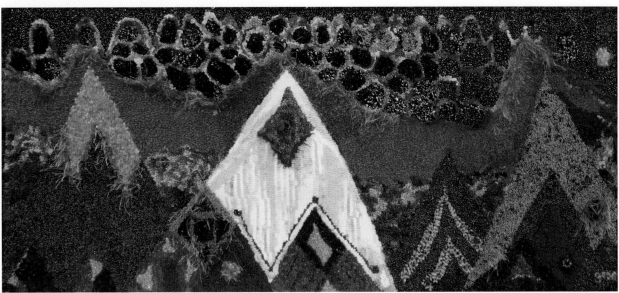

Vincent van Gogh to use cadmium yellow, a formula unavailable to painters from an earlier era. The hue and intensity of this color were new to the world of art in the latter part of the nineteenth century. People found the color shocking. But over the last century, the notion that certain colors are inherently good or bad in painting has disappeared; I would like to see strict adherence to such rules disappear from rug hooking, too.

COLOR BASICS

It is helpful to understand a smattering about basic color vocabulary and schemes.

■ Hue is any color other than black and white.

■ Chroma is the intensity of color saturation.

■ A shade is any hue mixed with black.

■ Tone is any hue mixed with gray.

■ Tint refers to any hue mixed with white (i.e., pink, because it is created by combining white and red). Colors that

Swiss Alps, 43" x 20", novelty fabrics, yarns, and ribbon on linen. Designed and hooked by Molly Dye, Jacksonville, Vermont, 2006.

Blue Pony, Color Study, 18" x 24", #6-cut hand-dyed wool on linen. Designed and hooked by Diane Kelly, Dorset Vermont, 2008.

Tree, 9" x 11", #6- and 7-cut as-is and over-dyed wool on linen. Designed and hooked by Diane Phillips, Fairport, New York, 2007. Extreme colors work because shapes, value, and scale are realistic.

are not mixed with white have a higher chroma than those that have been.

■ Value refers to the lightness and brightness of color.

Primary colors are red, blue, and yellow. By mixing any two of these colors together, you can create a secondary color.

■ Blue and yellow combine to create the secondary color green.

■ Red and yellow make orange.

■ Blue and red create violet.

Tertiary colors result by mixing one primary color with one secondary color.

■ Green and blue make aquamarine, or blue/green.

■ Red and orange make red/orange, and so on.

Complementary colors are opposite each other on the color wheel. If you put them side by side, their contrast is exciting. If you mix complementary colors in a dye pot, a neutral color results.

■ Red and green

■ Blue and orange

■ Yellow and purple

Don't worry if you find it difficult to remember all the facts about primary, secondary, and tertiary colors. You can always look up information on your color wheel, or use a search engine on your computer to study this on the Internet.

Four AM Milking (detail), #6-cut hand-dyed and over-dyed wool on linen. Designed and hooked by Diane Kelly, Dorset, Vermont, 2007. Simple shapes and high contrast are used to depict a night scene with distant evergreens against a snowy background. (See full rug on page 34.)

Field of Pussy Willows, 32" x 30", #3- ,4- , and 6-cut hand-dyed wool on linen. Designed and hooked by Linda Spear, Madison, New Hampshire, 2007. A cool background of blues and greens emphasizes the warmth of the pussy willow stalks. Note the unusual border within the composition. Gently flowing directional hooking of the background adds to the calming feel of this piece.

The Woman on the Swing, 29" x 44", #4- and 5-cut over-dyed and as-is wool on linen. Designed and hooked by Jen Lavoie, Huntington, Vermont, 2003. Warm colors attract the eye first. The viewer is immediately drawn to the red shawl, before exploring other elements of this poignant scene.

FOCUS ON VALUE

The most important point about color is that it has value, or qualities of light and dark. You are able to see one element separate from another because of contrast of value. When hooking a landscape, you want to keep values and shapes fairly realistic so the viewer understands what he or she is looking at. With hue, however, you can exaggerate to your heart's content. Diane Kelly's *Blue Pony Color Study* is a case in point. Even though it is blue, the creature whose head is hidden in the barn is clearly a pony or horse. Our brain allows us to interpret various realistic shapes and values so we are able to discern the pony from the barn from the fence from the foliage. Diane Phillip's *Tree* is hooked with hot pink and acid green. I've never seen a tree with bark in

Sunset, 29" x 16", #3- to 5-cut as-is, recycled, and over-dyed wool on linen. Designed and hooked by Jen Lavoie, Huntington, Vermont, 2006. Glowing warm backlights of a distant sunset and light-drenched field enhance the earth tones of tree trunks and forest shadows.

these hues, yet there is no question from the shape and striations of contrasting light and dark that this multicolored object represents a tree. The striations of bark would have been more difficult to detect if the tree had been hooked in multicolors of the same value.

How can you tell the value of an individual color? If this is not obvious to you, try my trick. I have a black and white photocopy of a color wheel I keep on hand. Blue/violet, violet, and red/violet have the darkest value. I can tell from my photocopied color-wheel because they read as the darkest shades of gray. Red, red/orange, and blue are of slightly lighter value (and a lighter shade of grey on the photocopy). Orange, blue/green, and green, are lighter still. Yellow/green is slightly lighter, and the color with the lightest and brightest value is yellow.

Practice discerning the different values of colored fiber. Go through your fiber horde and make piles of light-, medium-, and dark-valued wool of different colors. Check to see if you are accurate in your assessment by looking at your piles and squinting. Colors that seem to merge when you squint are closest in value to each other. Colors with the most contrast are the darkest and lightest. Another

trick is to look at your colored fiber through a red plastic lens that acts as a filter. Your fibers will all appear red, but you will be able to distinguish values of light, medium, and dark. Such lenses, made of red plastic, are inexpensive and available at photo supply stores.

COLOR TEMPERATURE

There are traditional notions matching color with temperature. For instance, blue is thought of as cold, perhaps because of its association with water and ice. Red is perceived as hot. (The irony is that the hottest of flames burn blue.) Warm colors (reds, oranges, yellows) attract the eye first. Thus, when initially viewing Jen Lavoie's *The Woman on the Swing,* your eye settles on the red shawl before moving on to the rest of the composition. Cool (blues, greens) or neutral (grays, beiges) colors seem to recede. A gradual graying and cooling of colors in a landscape suggest a gradual sense of space and depth.

If your scene depicts warm light on a figure or object, depict the shadow with a cool color. A warm palette of colors that are next to each other on the color wheel (called analogous colors) is thought to be restful to the eye. A monochromatic

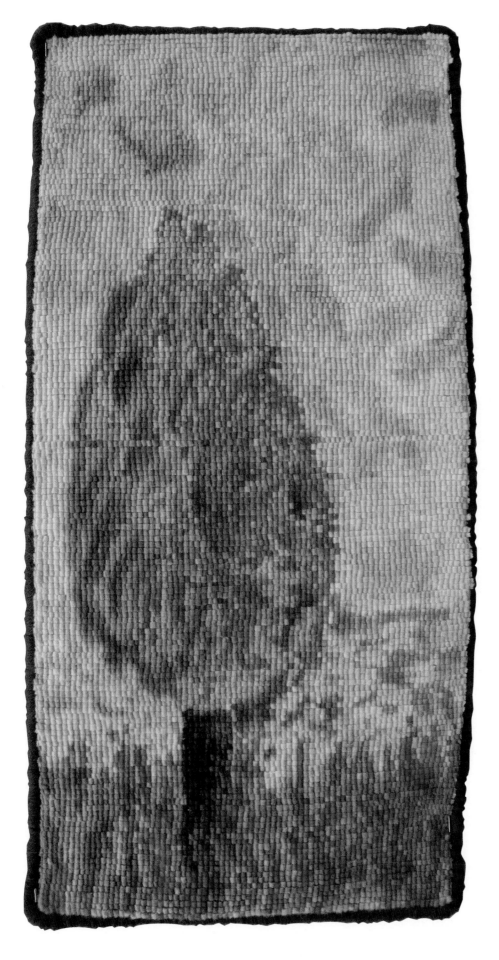

Dance in the Triumph of Summer, 13" x 26", #5-cut hand-painted wool on rug warp. Designed and hooked by Anne-Marie Littenberg, Burlington, Vermont, 2007. I worked with colors that are complements to my usual palette. Note the tree foliage is highlighted with a warm color (hot pink) to suggest the source of light comes from the right. The left, or shady side, is highlighted in cool blue.

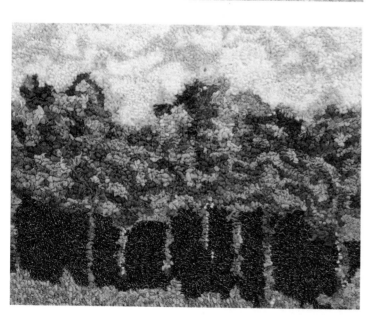

Tree Line I, II, III, three 14" x 11". Novelty fabrics, yarns, and ribbon on linen. Designed and hooked by Molly Dye, Jacksonville, Vermont, 2006. Hot, saturated pinks and oranges contrast with white and off-white.

palette, where the variation comes from value and intensity of color, is soothing when comprised of green and blue hues. Earth tones are beautifully enhanced by glowing warm backlights and highlights.

One of the big advantages contemporary rug hookers have over our forebears is our ability to exaggerate color temperature in our compositions. The innovation of safe acid dyes allows us to mix up colors that have extreme color temperatures in a way that could never have been achieved when rug hooking first evolved. Experiment with extremes of hue and color temperature, but remember to keep realistic tonal values in mind.

Dance in the Triumph of Summer represents my personal attempt at working with colors opposite my usual palette. How did I choose these colors? I photographed some of my older rugs, and then used a photo-editing program. This software allowed me to manipulate the pictures on my computer screen so I could convert the colors to their complements (or opposites on the color wheel). The hot pink, electric blue, and burning orange in this rug are not found in any grass and tree foliage I know of in nature. Yet, the values in the piece are fairly realistic, so the viewer is able to understand I was trying to depict a tree on grass, surrounded by a colorful sky. Note that the right side of the tree trunk is lighter in value than the left. This shading helps to impart a sense that the light is coming from the right. The yellow in the sky and hot pink reflected on the right side of the treetop add to the notion that the light is coming from the right. The sky is cooler on the left, and the values of the tree suggest that is its shady side.

Too Cold to Skate (detail), hand-cut over-dyed wool on rug warp. Designed and hooked by Jule Marie Smith, Ballston Spa, New York, 1994. The warm glow of fire and eye-popping small touches of red in the skaters' accessories contrast with the cold blues and off-whites of snow and ice. (See full rug on page 2.)

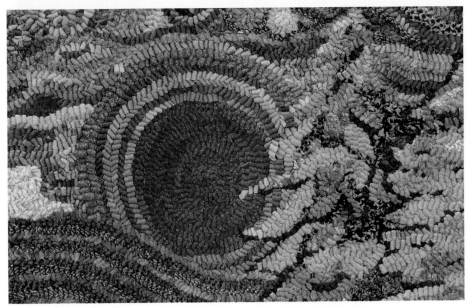

Hinesburg, Vermont (detail), #6-, 7-, and 8-cut over-dyed and as-is wool on monk's cloth. Designed and hooked by Rae Harrell, Hinesburg, Vermont, 2002. An explosion of different colors and textures are used in the sun and evergreen trees. From the collection of Ramsey Yoder. (See full rug on page 20.)

CHOOSING COLOR

How should you choose color for your hooked rug landscape? What colors are you drawn to? What colors do you hate? Are you willing to venture outside your comfort zone? Two colors I use most frequently in my palette are variations of green and purple. Until a few years ago, I detested these colors. A friend urged me to experiment with them to see if I could figure out the source of my intense dislike. The outcome was that I now continually gravitate toward them.

Do you want your rug to pop with bright, intense color, or are you looking for something with more of a neutral palette? Are you willing to experiment with the dye pot? What colors do you have on hand? Are you trying to match the décor of a room? (I urge you to expand your creative horizon far beyond interior design. The best art comes from the artists' heart, and not from drapes or upholstery.) Try these tips and tricks.

1. Play with your own instinct about color and try to liberate yourself from anyone else's rules of right and wrong.

2. Remember that color is informed by what is around it. Thus, a piece of green wool will look very different when it is laid

Cityscape, 21" x 14", #4-cut hand-dyed wool, hand-spun yarn, and novelty yarn on linen. Designed and hooked by Molly Colegrove, Canandaigua, New York, 2008. Molly wanted the challenge of hooking a rug in shades of gray. Novelty yarn add specks of color.

Summerfields, 26" x 22", #6-cut hand-dyed wool on monk's cloth. Designed and hooked by Anne-Marie Littenberg, Burlington, Vermont, 2005. A single shade of light green is used in every element of Summerfields.

next to a piece of orange or brown wool. Pull out bunches of fiber and scrunch them up into piles on the floor. Stand back and look. Take pictures of different fabric combinations and look at them on the computer.

3. Look at your color choices in different light. Varying conditions affect how you will perceive color. Direct sunlight and incandescent bulbs add a yellow cast to your fiber. Florescent bulbs add a blue quality. Indirect natural light will give you the most accurate representation of your color. Look at your fabric outside on a bright, overcast day.

4. Find a painting or photo you love, and study the colors you see. Look carefully at every inch of the image, and pick out the subtle use of color. Make a list of the different colors and values. Then, figure out how much of each color is used in rela-

tion to the other colors. Do you see any colors you have never worked with before? Do you notice any surprise color combinations you were not expecting? This exercise may help you to see that you don't necessarily need a lot of different colors in your hooked rug landscape. Also, colors you thought didn't match might work well as highlights, shadows, and more.

5. If you choose to work with a lot of pure colors, think about using them to varying degrees; choose one color to dominate your plan.

6. Make it work! I believe you can make any color satisfactory as long as it is the right value and distributed in a balanced way throughout the composition. How can you achieve this look? I like to literally scatter loops from a single piece of wool throughout my rug, trying to distribute it through multiple elements in the

Boathouses, 24" x 19", #5- to 7-cut hand-dyed and over-dyed recycled wool on linen. Designed and hooked by Molly Colegrove, Canandaigua, New York, 2005. Molly wanted to create a rug that looked like an oil painting. Note the reflection of the boathouses in the water. A cool palette provides strong contrast to saturated reds.

Twilight in Vermont,
26" x 19", #4- and 6-cut hand-dyed and as-is wool on rug warp. Designed and hooked by Betty Bouchard, Richmond, Vermont, 2004. Do purple, red, and orange clash? Not when used judiciously, as demonstrated here. The strong red of the barn and purple of the sky work with the tiny orange highlights in the foliage shown on the left. This combination excites an otherwise neutral palette.

composition. *Summerfields* has a shade of light green that is used in every element in the rug. It is in the round ball of the sun and scattered throughout the sky. It is also deployed in small flecks in the three mountains, the tree foliage, the mid-ground field, and the foreground foliage. In the tree foliage, I scattered strips, hooking four or five loops before cutting the wool and moving on to another little bit of foliage. In the sky, the strips were scattered in strings of 10 to 12 loops.

Distributing the same wool in every element may be extreme. A simple, old-fashioned rule of thumb is to try and use a color in at least three places in your composition.

7. Dye your own! Dyeing wool is like cooking. When you are first learning, all you have to do is get the right ingredients and follow the recipe. It's easier than cooking in that a botched dinner may be inedible, but the wrong color wool can always be over dyed.

I am a big fan of learning dye formulas based on the three primary colors (red, blue, and yellow) with tiny additions of black. Any and every color you come up with from various combinations of a few initial dyes will go with every other color you create from those same supplies because they share the same pigments, just in different ratios.

8. Copy! Color palettes are not copyrighted, so go ahead and copy color combinations you admire from any and every source you can think of such as fashion and decorating magazines, swatches of silk prints, a favorite painting, or the colors in a quilt.

COLOR TOOLS

Take advantage of a variety of tools to help with your color selections

Teleidescope. This device looks like a kaleidoscope, but a clear marble occupies one end of its tube rather than a chamber filled with broken glass. The marble serves

as a lens so that when you view your wool, it shows the different colors combined in kaleidoscope-like patterns. You can quickly tell how your colors will combine, if one will stand out over the others, and whether sufficient variation in value exists. This tool is a popular device among quilters.

Paint Chips. A trip to the paint department of the hardware store provides a wealth of color possibilities. Collect the paint chips people use to help select colors for their homes. Mix and match the colors to see how you feel about the different combinations.

Dye Swatches. Invest in the dye swatches from a dyer whose color sense you admire, and then use your own eye to decide which color selections will best fit your purpose. I find this kind of eye matching to be much easier than trying to remember rules of color theory. If you stick with the swatches from a single dyer's palette, they will always work together. Then, when you find a color you like, you

can easily reproduce it by just following the accompanying dye recipe. As you gain dyeing experience, you will also gain confidence in your own abilities, and eventually you will develop your own series of dye formulas and color palettes.

Your Brain. Your own brain is your most valuable tool. It has been working with color your entire life. You think of color when you dress in the morning, and when you decorate a room. Trust your instinct. Worry more about using the right value. If you are timid about moving beyond your color comfort zone, try introducing one new color to your already-established palette. Work with it until you are used to it, and then add another color.

Vermont Vignette, 14" x 12", #3-, 4-, and 6-cut hand-dyed and as-is wool on monk's cloth. Designed and hooked by Betty Bouchard, Richmond, Vermont, 2003. Betty Bouchard is masterful at hooking snow, showing that the traditional rule of never using white can be broken. She combines myriad subtle shades and directional hooking to achieve her frosty effects. I once asked her how she hooks snow and she said, "I just pull strips from my snow bag."

CHAPTER 7

Hooking your Composition

You've designed your landscape, and you are ready to hook. Where should you start? This subject is deeply informed by personal preference and methods that work for one person may not be acceptable for another. I'll describe my own process.

I always start with the element I find most challenging. If my composition includes a person, that's where I begin. If there is no person, then I commence with the most dominant, clearly distinct element, such as a tree. The size, position, color, and value choices that go into a figure, or your most dominant element, are very impor-

Purple Mountains Majesty, 14" x 15", various plied threads of linen, silk, cotton, polyester, wool, etc. on rug warp. Designed and hooked by Anne-Marie Littenberg, Burlington, Vermont, 2005.

Fall Reflection (detail), #3-, 4-, and 5-cut hand-dyed, as-is, over-dyed, and hand-painted wool on linen. Designed and hooked by Jen Lavoie, Huntington, Vermont, 2006. Many small strips of wool, hooked in strings of five or six loops at a time, result in beautiful fall foliage. Note that the slender tree trunks are hooked in the direction they grow in nature. Colors from the trees are repeated on the ground. (See full rug on page 83.)

tant to the placement of everything else in your composition. By starting with the most challenging element, I can conquer the part of the project that embodies my deepest concerns, getting the hardest of it out of the way first.

Hook your loops so they mimic the flow found in nature. Thus, I tend to hook tree trunks from the ground up. I start with the trunk, and then move on to the foliage. When hooking the foliage, keep in mind where you imagine your source of light to be. Does one side of the treetop need highlighting? Should the leaves closer to the trunk be darker to indicate shading?

After the tree is in place, I will hook a horizon line, or the line where the

The Woman on the Swing (detail), #4- and 5-cut over-dyed and as-is wool on linen. Designed and hooked by Jen Lavoie, Huntington, Vermont, 2003. The whorls, swirls, and loops of browns, grays, and tweed provide an excellent lesson in how to hook tree bark. (See full rug on page 63.)

ground meets distant mountains. I then move on to foreground foliage. The colors and value of foreground foliage and tree leaves are most saturated and bright. As a field moves off into the distance, the colors become less saturated and duller, helping to create the illusion of the land receding into the distance.

If my composition involves mountains, I move on to them next. I like multiple layers of mountains. The closest mountain will be darker and brighter than the mountains that recede. Try using the colors and values of your closest ground foliage in your closest mountain. The second distant mountain may have colors and values from the mid- or far-ground of your receding field. Your most distant mountain will have the lightest values of all. Another trick for achieving a sense of something receding is to use larger cuts of wool in your foreground and smaller cuts for elements in the distance.

Sky and water are my favorite things to hook. I love to take colors from the rest of the composition and swirl them in

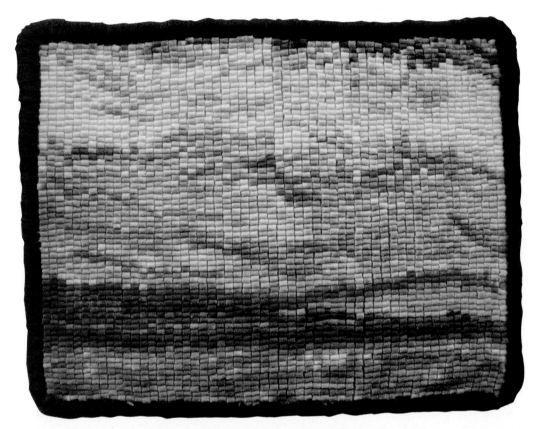

Rosey Fingered Dawn, 15" x 11", #7-cut hand-painted wool on monk's cloth. Designed and hooked by Anne-Marie Littenberg, Burlington, Vermont, 2007. The title, with its misspelled "rosey," comes from nineteenth-century translations of both "The Iliad" and "The Odyssey" by Homer. Sunrise is depicted by horizontal bands of color.

Burning Kisses of the Sun, 19" x 14", #4-cut hand-painted wool on linen. Designed and hooked by Anne-Marie Littenberg, Burlington, Vermont, 2007. A setting sun is shown with color transitioning from warm on the left to cool on the right.

Shiva Meditating in the Forest, 31" x 31", #6- to 8-cut as-is and over-dyed wool, novelty yarns and fabrics, and hand beading on monk's cloth. Designed and hooked by Rae Harrell, Hinesburg, Vermont, 2007.

We rug hookers have traditionally worked primarily with pure wool that has been cut into strips. Wool has extraordinary body and strength and can stand up to years of foot traffic. It dyes beautifully, allowing enormous creative expression through the dye pot. What happens when a rug hooker defies the boundaries of tradition, employing new and unusual materials in their hooked rug landscapes?

The effect can be stunning. Keep in mind that when rug hooking first evolved, materials were chosen from whatever scraps the crafter might have had on hand. Wool is so durable, that it has stood the test of time and evolved into the preferred material of choice. However, the history of rug hooking tells us that creative use of any available material is well within the traditional boundaries of the craft. I think of rug hooking as art. And as artists, we should be encouraged to explore moving past traditional boundaries.

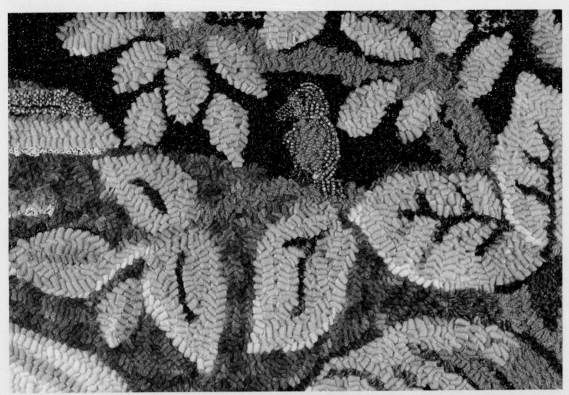

Shiva Meditating in the Forest (detail). Beads add sparkle to the nested bird.

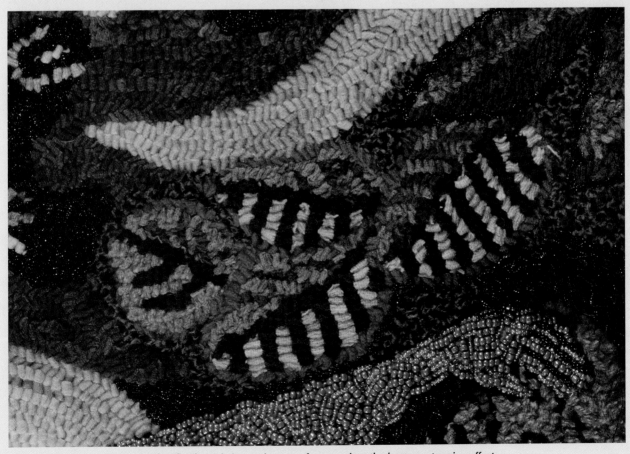

Shiva Meditating in the Forest (detail). The artist's creative use of scraps gives the leaves a stunning effect.

Espagna, 33" x 30", novelty fabrics, yarns, and ribbon on linen. Designed and hooked by Molly Dye, Jacksonville, Vermont, 2007.

Broken (triptych detail), three 18" x 24" panels, various wool, silk, and cotton yarns, threads, and cut Mylar on linen. Designed and hooked by Anne-Marie Littenberg, Burlington, Vermont, 2003. The full rug can be viewed on page 88-89.

Rae Harrell added sparkle and pizzazz to her rug titled, *Shiva in the Forest,* when she used fine beading for the foliage-nestled bird. I experimented with wool yarns, thread, and strips of cut Mylar in my 9/11 mourning piece titled, *Broken.* Molly Dye, who earned her McGowan credentials years ago, uses all manner of fabric other than wool in her hooking. I remember a fabric shopping trip to the textile district in Montreal, Canada, where she asked that I bring back "anything, gaudy, sparkly, and over the top." Do you have a long-discarded, sad bridesmaid or prom dress? Do the 1980s still live in the back of

your closet? If so, you may have a treasure trove of interesting material for a new hooked rug.

Keep the following notes in mind when using unusual materials in a hooked rug:

1. Fragile fabric and embellishments work well on a hooked rug landscape created solely for the purpose of display. They do not stand up well to foot traffic. Stick with pure wool if you plan to use your rug on the floor.

2. Contemporary, unusual fabrics generally have a low melting point. Take enormous care when pressing your rug. I suggest keeping some scraps to test under the iron. I also keep a separate iron, solely for pressing unusual materials, in case of a meltdown. Also, be sure to use a pressing cloth to protect your materials.

3. Materials other than wool can be rough on a cutter blade.

Consider cutting manmade materials with a hand-held rotary blade, or a scissor.

4. Gauzy, light fabrics can pose challenges when hooking. I like to use a double width strip that has been folded over to give the loops more body.

5. Unusual materials may not travel well with your hooked rug. For instance, some materials may flatten when the rug is rolled up for storage or shipping. Consider laying a sheet of muslin over your rug before rolling it for storage. If the loops are flattened when you take the rug out, gently run your fingers over the fibers to coax them back into the desired shape.

6. When I make a rug from materials other than wool strips, I line the back of the rug to provide further protection over time.

Foggy Marsh, 26" x 19", #4- and 5-cut hand-dyed wool and hand-spun and commercial yarns on linen. Designed and hooked by Molly Colegrove, Canandaigua, New York, 2005. Based on a 1985 photo taken by the artist, Molly captures the effects of fog using fuzzy fibers.

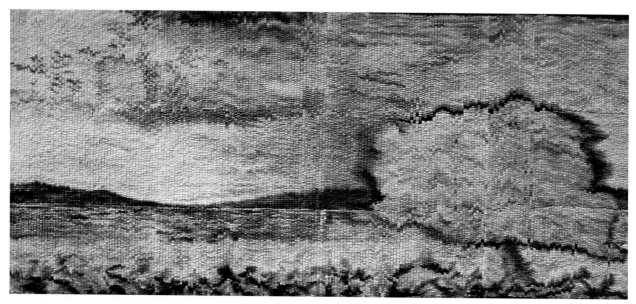

While the Season of Spring Comes On, 55" x 28", #6-cut hand-painted wool on monk's cloth. Designed and hooked by Anne-Marie Littenberg, Burlington, Vermont, 2007. The sky has blue from the water, and green, yellow, and purple from the foreground foliage and tree. The distant shore, tree foliage outline and trunk are the same charcoal.

the sky. I always hook the sky before water. Sky is where I allow myself to be the most instinctual in my artistic decisions. Study the color and value of the land and mountains you have already hooked, and see if you have included shadows (such as shade under a tree or shaded sides of fence posts). This will help you determine where the light is coming from in the sky.

Rug hookers often choose to depict dramatic sunrises or sunsets with bands of color that begin at the horizon and work up to the heavens. This technique works

nicely. However, look out at a sunset one evening and move your eye toward the north or south. Note that color transitions from left to right too as you move away from the light source (the sun). I like to depict this transition, hooking a sky so that warm hues on the left transition to cool hues on the right. It adds an unexpected element of interest to the composition.

If you are working from a photograph and trying to reproduce a specific sky, keep in mind the photo will appear lighter than the actual sky because of

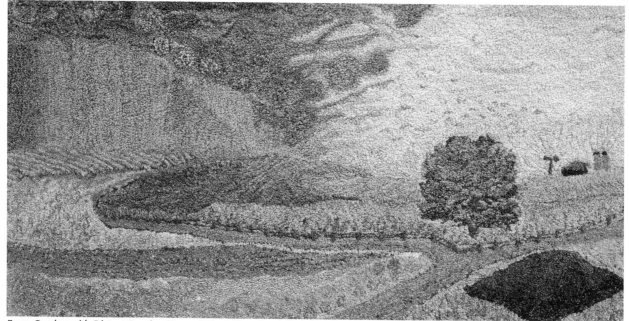

Farm Garden with Distant Passing Storm, 39" x 21", various plied threads of silk, cotton, wool, rayon, polyester, etc. on cotton rug warp. Designed and hooked by Anne-Marie Littenberg, Burlington, Vermont, 2004; from the collection of Diane Kelly.

Salisbury Plane, 32" x 25", novelty fabrics, yarns, and ribbon on linen. Designed and hooked by Molly Dye, Jacksonville, Vermont, 2005. Dramatic, abstract shapes and swirls form the sky.

Sailboats, 27" x 22", #4-, 5- and 6-cut recycled, over-dyed, and marbleized wool on linen. Designed and hooked by Molly Colegrove, Canandaigua, New York, 2005. Hooked entirely from old skirts that were bright pink, green, and blue. Molly marbleized them with different off-white wools, resulting in a variety of soft colors.

Sailboats (detail). Note the hull reflected in the water.

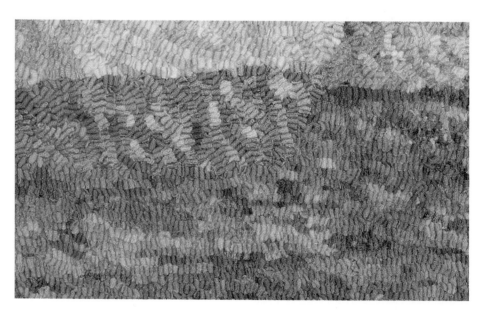

how the camera adjusts for light. Notice that the real sky is not always blue. During the day, the color of the sky on the horizon tends to be of much lighter value than the sky overhead.

Depict weather variations in your sky using directional hooking. *Farm Garden* shows a rainstorm on the left. This weather event is depicted by straight loops that angle to mimic rainfall. They are topped by swirls of loops that suggest storm clouds. The storm has not yet hit the right side of the composition, so the sky is still light blue and you can see sunset beyond the red barn and silos.

If water is included in my composition, it is the last thing I hook. Water reflects the colors of the sky and surrounding landscape. If water sits in front of mountains, or has a shoreline, the water's edge includes a scattering of loops from those elements. If the water reflects the sky, it is hooked in the same colors, but of a much more intense value. Scatter loops to give the illusion of light reflected from the moon or sun.

Fall Reflection, 20" x 25", #3-, 4-, and 5-cut hand-dyed, as-is, over-dyed, and hand-painted wool on linen. Designed and hooked by Jen Lavoie, Huntington, Vermont, 2006. Fall foliage is reflected in the water. The reflection is hooked with wool hand-painted with dyes used in the fall foliage.

I Was Like a Watcher of the Skies,
12" x 14", #4-cut hand-painted wool on
monk's cloth. Designed and hooked by
Anne-Marie Littenberg, Burlington,
Vermont, 2007. Striations of light in the
water are a mirror image of light in the
sky. The colors of the water are the same as the
sky but more intensely saturated.

The Sun Poured Over the Golden Day,
14" x 15", #4-cut hand-painted wool on
monk's cloth. Designed and hooked by
Anne-Marie Littenberg, Burlington,
Vermont, 2007. Water reflects the dark
shoreline and all the colors of the sky. Dark
streaks are the same color as the far shore.
Their diagonal line suggests rippling water.

Eve in the Garden of Eden, 57" x 32", #7-cut over-dyed and hand-dyed wool on linen. Hooked and designed by Diane Phillips, Fairport, New York, 2005. The foliage comes from Diane's imagination. She was not hampered by worrying about botanical reality. The angular shapes in the leaves of the plant in the lower left foreground mimic the patterning of the serpent. Eve's skin tones reflect the colors of the many peoples of the world.

When hooking a large body of water that meets a distant shoreline, I highlight that shore with a single, straight line in a lighter value than either the land or the water. Look at a distant shore the next time you are near a large body of water, and you will see this illusion exists in nature, too.

Create recognizable, but abstracted elements. Your foliage does not have to be realistic. You can make up trees and plants that exist only in your imagination, as Diane Phillips did in *Eve in the Garden of Eden.*

Look beyond the world of hooked rug art to discover and develop techniques

Let's Play in the Moonlight (detail), various plied threads of linen, silk, cotton, polyester, wool, etc. on verel. Designed and hooked by Anne-Marie Littenberg, Burlington, Vermont, 2005; from the collection of Sharon Townsend. A variety of blues and purples scatter the night sky, framing the moon. (See full rug on page 4.)

that will enhance your landscapes. The goal of landscape painters through the earlier parts of the nineteenth century, especially before the advent of photography, was to create pictures that were accurate visual renditions of a view. The French Impressionists shocked the world with their vision of landscapes in pigment-drenched, hot, complementary colors laid down with strong, bold brush strokes. Study the works of painters whose individual brush strokes can be discerned on their canvasses. See how the direction of brush strokes adds to your understanding of what the painter is trying to depict, such as a field of wheat or a swirling sky. Mimic those brush strokes with your strips of fiber. Mix in a variety of materials in different cut sizes.

Have you ever watched a painter working on a canvas? Notice how he or she will lay down slashes and blobs of

Towers Barn, 26" x 19", #4- to 6-cut hand-painted, over-dyed, and as-is wool on linen. Designed and hooked by Jen Lavoie, Huntington, Vermont, 2005. The flat gray of the sky and distant mountains provide a backdrop for detailed foreground foliage.

Towers Barn (detail). Subtle outlining and directional hooking distinguish the fence posts from the foreground foliage.

Sky Swirls, 29" x 24", novelty fabrics, yarns, and ribbon on linen. Designed and hooked by Molly Dye, Jacksonville, Vermont, 2005. Molly Dye's exuberant designs reflect self-confidence in her work.

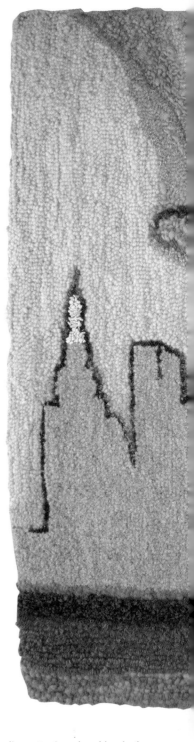

Broken (triptych), each panel is 18" x 24", various wool, silk, and cotton yarns, threads, and cut Mylar on linen. Designed and hooked by Anne-Marie Littenberg, Burlington, Vermont, 2003, from the collection of Rae Harrell. This is my 9/11 mourning piece. I was compelled to do it for personal reasons, even though it generated a lot of negative response. If my work moves people to a passionate response, whether positive or negative, I feel I have succeeded.

color all over the canvas. This painting technique is markedly different from how we tend to hook our rugs. Our rugs tend to be hooked so that solid areas of hooked blocks and blobs emerge. Con-

sider trying to work all over the backing, laying down loops and color the way a painter lays down pigment. For example, when hooking grass, I will start with one color and scatter a few dozen blades of

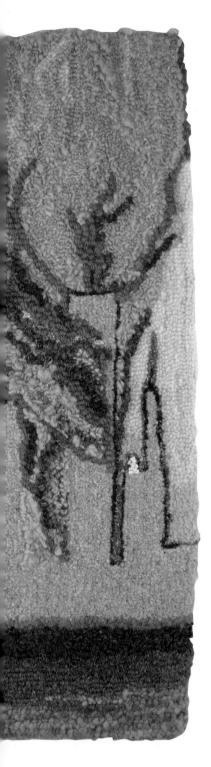

grass around the foreground of my backing. They initially look like lonely ribbons of wool. I then go back with a different color and value that provides some contrast and scatter those strips of loops about the backing. Some of these strips of wool are contiguous to others. Many are not. This process is repeated a third time with a third color and value. Finally, I fill the space between the dis-

tinct blades of grass with whatever I choose to complete the foreground.

THE ARTIST'S ATTITUDE

Here are my personal guidelines. I urge you to consider them as you begin working on your hooked rug landscapes:

1. Do not make self-deprecating comments about your work. I have rarely met a rug hooker who responds with a plain

Summer Scene and *Winter Scene*, each panel is 28" x 22", #3- and 4-cut hand-dyed and as-is wool. Summer is on linen; winter, on burlap. Designed with help from Marjorie Judson. Hooked by Betty Bouchard, Richmond, Vermont, 1988. Subtle changes in composition and color distinguish the same view of a town in different seasons.

and simple, "thank you," when their work is admired. We all tend to immediately deprecate our work, pointing out to the viewer what we did wrong and opining about how someone else does it better. Cut it out! Say thank you, and believe it!

2. Ask questions. There is no such thing as a stupid question or observation. As you take classes, discuss art with your friends, and get together to hook with your fiber art community, ask questions and make observations. Do not worry about whether or not you should or shouldn't speak up. If anyone discourages you from doing this, it is a reflection on him or her and not of the value of your query. Your thoughts are important!

3. Be fearless in your work. What is the worst thing that can happen? Maybe you'll hook something that displeases you and you'll either ban the piece to a closet,

or tear it out and redo it. Revel in the joy of the process of artistic discovery and creation. Remember that even the most accomplished rug hookers have mistakes stored deep in the back of a closet somewhere. Don't worry about failure. Life is too short.

4. Learn the established rules of rug hooking, and then experiment by breaking them. I am a self-taught rug hooker. When I finally learned the rules, I wished I had known them all along because they would have saved me a ton of time and effort, not to mention expense. But now that I know them, it is great fun to break them. Many rules are essential for specific applications. For instance, if you plan to use your rug on the floor, the traditional rules about crossovers and finishing techniques are important for how your work will survive the test of time. But if you

plan to exclusively display your work on the wall, you can enjoy tremendous freedom in your decisions about what materials to use and which finishing techniques to employ. Knowing rules about artistic decisions (such as whether you should use certain color combinations) will be helpful if you then go on to break them. Vincent van Gogh, Rembrandt van Rijn, and Pablo Picasso broke the rules all the time. If they could do it, why can't you?

5. Suffering doesn't improve your art. I have watched too many hooked rug fiber artists slave over work they just don't care for. If you are working on a project and it is making you miserable, put it away. Look at it again in a few months or a year. If you decide you do not want to complete it, move on to something else.

6. Van Gogh has all the answers. (You can substitute your own favorite artist for rule #6). Whenever I am puzzled by how to choose a color, place a figure, or hook a sky, I skim through art books. Looking at the work of other artists can give you insight about color, composition, value, directional hooking, and much more. Van Gogh is my favorite painter. I learned from him that color doesn't matter as much as value. He was very poor, and the colors he chose for his work often depended on what he had on hand. He didn't have the money to go out and buy the additional pigments he might have preferred. Using only what he had readily available, he created work that moves me. The color choices he employed often bore no resemblance to those found in nature, and yet, they worked.

The Apple (border detail), #6- and 8-cut over-dyed and as-is wool on monk's cloth. Designed and hooked by Rae Harrell, Hinesburg, Vermont, 2002. (See full rug on page 6.)

To me, borders are one of the great hooked rug mysteries. I haven't found a way to incorporate elaborate borders in my own work in a way that is pleasing. When viewing hooked rugs, I sometimes find a border to be distracting, overbearing, and just plain wrong. Rug hookers are taught to contain their work with a border. When this works well, it is a beautiful thing. But sometimes the border looks slapped on and unrelated to the composition, as if the rug hooker was told that a border was essential but didn't understand how to make it an integral, complimentary part of the design.

Luckily, the world of rug hooking includes some people who do extraordinary borders. I love the way Rae Harrell uses the edge of her rugs as another opportunity for inventive, exuberant design. Sometimes her borders weave in and out among the central design elements of her rugs. I also love that she is not married to the idea that her rug edge must be a straight line.

Jule Marie Smith's borders frame and compliment her rugs. They are so gorgeously executed that they can stand on their own as individual works of art. Jen Lavoie's borders can, from a

distance, seem to be elegantly simple. Closer study, however, shows that subtle variations in color, texture, and value gently draw the viewer into the rug.

Diane Kelly's borders are neat as a pin. Note on the detail photo of *Color Study: Blue Barn,* that her rug's edge is covered with wool leftover from her hooking. She achieves this result by covering her cording with wool, in the same way an upholsterer covers cording on a sofa cushion's edge. The color of each part of the edging matches the wool in the contiguous hooking. The border is a crisp, continuation of the composition of the rug.

When designing a border, please keep the following notes in mind.

1. The material in your border should also be used in other parts of the rug. Think carefully before introducing a new color or texture to the rug by placing it only in the border. You want the border to look as though it was designed in a way that enhances the subject matter and individual elements of your hooked rug landscape.

2. Remember that whatever wool you put in the border will instantly emphasize the other places in the rug where that wool is used.

Hinesburg, Vermont (border detail), #6-, 7-, and 8-cut over-dyed and as-is wool on monk's cloth. Designed and hooked by Rae Harrell, Hinesburg, Vermont, 2002; from the collection of Ramsey Yoder. (See full rug on page 20.)

Corn (border detail), 33" x 62", #3- to 6-cut as-is, over-dyed, and hand-painted wool on linen. Designed and hooked by Jen Lavoie, Huntington, Vermont, 2007. (See full rug on page 53.)

Too Cold to Skate (border detail), hand-cut over-dyed wool on rug warp. Designed and hooked by Jule Marie Smith, Ballston Spa, New York, 1994. (See full rug on page 2.)

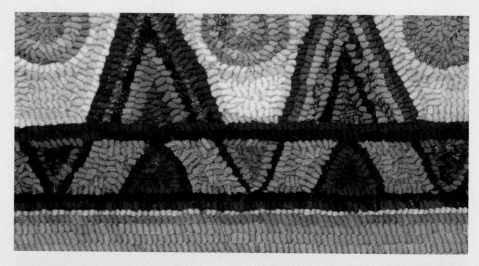

Blue Barn, Color Study (border detail), #6-cut hand-dyed wool on linen. Designed and hooked by Diane Kelly, Dorset, Vermont, 2008. (See full rug on page 58.)

3. Don't choose a fabric for the border just because you have the leftovers lying around.

4. Consider the proportions of your border. I have seen delicately hooked, beautifully designed scenes framed by heavy, dark borders. If the border is very heavy and of significantly darker value than the rest of the rug, the viewer's eye may focus on the border and be distracted from the subject.

5. Sometimes people choose to use formal carved wood picture frames for their hooked rug art. I have seen this work with and without success. I've seen rugs where the wood frame provides a neat, containing edge. I've also seen rugs where the quality of the work in the frame is out of proportion to the hooking. When this happens, the viewer's eye is drawn to the frame instead of the hooking. Do not put a frame of inferior or superior quality on your work.

6. When you glance at a rug, do you first notice the frame, border, or hooking? What do you want the viewer to notice first?

7. When in doubt, do without. If it is not obvious to you how to design an elaborate border to enhance your rug, consider finishing it with a simple, whipped edge. Resist advice from friends and associates who insist you must have a border if it doesn't feel right and natural to you.

8. If you do wish to create an elaborate border, ask yourself what problem you are trying to solve by adding this to the rug.

9. Consider having design elements, such as leaves or creatures, from your hooked rug landscape spilling over into the border.

CHAPTER 8

Evaluating Your Work

How often do you complete a rug and find it doesn't satisfy you? Rug hookers frequently design a pattern, transfer it to their backing, make color and material selections, and then adhere to their original game plan in completing the rug. It is as if all the creative and artistic choices have been inalterably settled once the hooking begins. However, constant evaluation of a work in progress can help the rug hooker understand what does and does not achieve the desired effects.

Review the progress of your work as you go through the process of designing, hooking, and redesigning your

Distant Pandemonium of the Sun, 11" x 15", #6-cut hand-painted wool on monk's cloth. Designed and hooked by Anne-Marie Littenberg, Burlington, Vermont, 2007. How a rug appears changes dramatically when viewed from a distance. This rug is more successful when viewed from across a room rather than up close.

Canyon de Chelly (detail), #3- to 5-cut as-is, recycled, and hand-painted wool on linen. Designed and hooked by Jen Lavoie, Huntington, Vermont, 2007. Jen is rigorous in evaluating and editing her work. She re-hooked this figure multiple times before completing the rug. She depends on her friend Polly Alexander to provide thoughtful and effective feedback. (See full rug on page 48.)

landscape. How can you tell if the composition works, or if your value choices and perspective make the piece understandable? Will others be able to discern what you are trying to accomplish? You work on your rug up close, on a frame or in your lap. When the finished product is viewed, however, it will often be from a distance. What you see in your lap, under your lamp, and with your reading glasses, may vary greatly from what one would see from across a room or while looking down at the floor. The effects of light, contrast, shading, and perspective change dramatically with distance.

Jen Lavoie puts extraordinary effort into getting her work just right. She re-hooked the figure of the girl wrapped in a blanket in *Canyon de Chelly* six times before she was satisfied. The girl is a tiny part of the composition, but for Jen, attention to detail is an essential element of her artistry. Rug hookers who create great pieces do so through constant work, evaluation, and re-hooking. A perfect piece doesn't just spring magically from the artist's hands. Are you willing to redo areas of your rug if your initial effort does not satisfy you? Here are some tips and tricks to help you check your work in progress.

Ask Me Anything, 28" x 19", various plied threads of linen, silk, cotton, polyester, wool, etc. on verel. Designed and hooked by Anne-Marie Littenberg, Burlington, Vermont, 2006. I did not realize the figure of the woman was distorted until I viewed this rug on a computer screen.

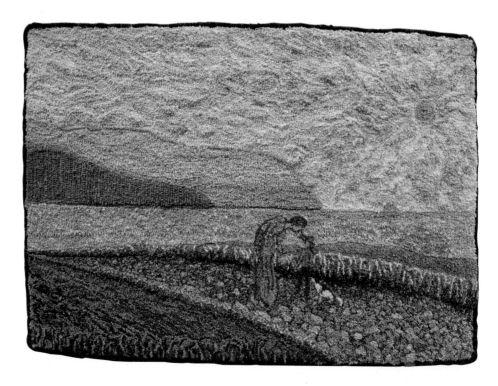

Too Cold to Skate (details), hand-cut over-dyed wool on rug warp. Designed and hooked by Jule Marie Smith, Ballston Spa, New York, 1994. Photo editing software allows rug hookers to enlarge minute details of a work to evaluate the success of the design and execution. (See full rug on page 2.)

1. Step away from your work. Every day you work on your rug, take time to view it from a distance. Have a friend or family member hold up your rug from across the room so you can view it. Or, place it at the bottom of the steps in your home. View the rug from the top of the steps. When I am uncertain about the progress of a piece, I will leave it at the bottom of the steps for several days so I can see it over a period of time and study the different effects of light and distance.

2. Use your camera. Photograph your rug at different stages of progress and look at the images on a computer. For some mysterious reason, your eye will see things on the computer screen that you don't see in real time. For example, the figure of the woman bending over a boy in my rug, *Ask me Anything,* is distorted. Until I saw her on the computer screen, I did not realize she was hunch-backed and proportioned like someone walking on stilts. The lower half of her body should be about forty percent shorter than it is.

When viewing your rug on the computer screen, use the gray scale function on a photo editor. This option allows you to view your rug as a black and white photo. Turning the image to gray scale will help detect if you are employing sufficient contrast in your fiber selections. Subtleties of shading and transition of elements will disappear or distort in gray scale if your value choices don't work.

3. Mirrors. Stand in front of a mirror, holding your rug in front of you. What do

you see? The mirror, like the computer screen, will help you see things you won't normally detect.

SOLICITING FEEDBACK

Does your piece work if you have to explain it to another? Does it bother you if your cousin thinks your darling kitten is a cute raccoon? Are you satisfied if your husband thinks the barn is an interesting mountain? And yet, when we ask the question, "What do you think?" we always seem to get exuberant, positive feedback ("That's darling!").

Family and friends may be shy about providing unadorned critiques of our work. Also, we may be reluctant to hear anything but praise. Consider working with a close group of your rug hooking colleagues to build a relationship where together you can develop a vehicle for effective feedback.

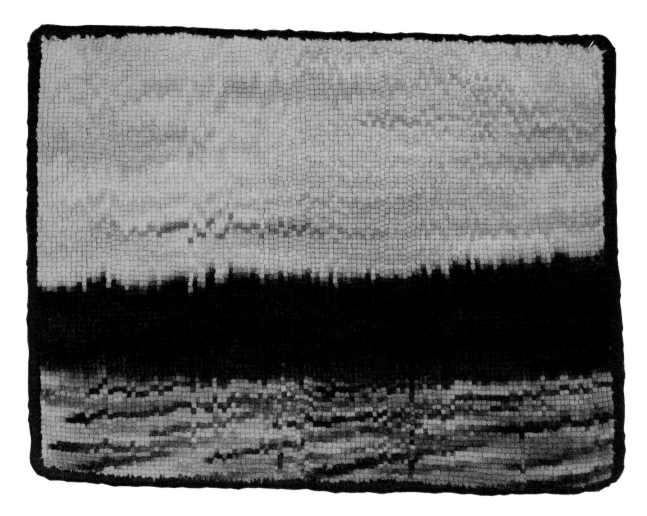

Dawn Put Fire in the Sky, 17" x 13", #3-cut hand-painted wool on rug warp. Designed and hooked by Anne-Marie Littenberg, Burlington, Vermont, 2007.

Blue Pony, Color Study (detail), #6-cut hand-dyed wool on linen. Designed and hooked by Diane Kelly, Dorset Vermont, 2008. Diane and I belong to a study group where we provide serious feedback about our work. I asked Diane why the pony's head was hidden in the barn. She laughed and said, "This is just a color study. I thought the head would be too hard to hook." (See full rug on page 60.)

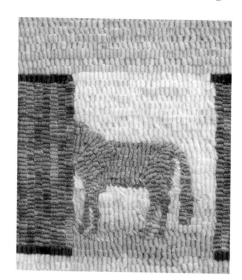

Giving and receiving effective feedback is a learned process. It is not about just saying what you think. It can be exceedingly challenging when you embark on your first round of critiques. However, it gets easier within a very short period of time. Successful and effective feedback depends on the following:

1. All participants must share a strong sense of trust. Everyone must be equally willing to both provide and receive feedback.

2. Comments must be honest and about the work not the worker. This forum is not the place for providing editorials about personal likes and dislikes. It is all right to say, "The whipping on your edge is uneven, detracting from the overall quality of your work." It is not all right to say, "You are sloppy."

3. Comments should be specific and backed up by thoughtful reasoning. "I like the rug," is nice to hear but not helpful. "Your rug depicts bright sunlight, but there is no shading under that tree. Adding shadows might help anchor the piece," is helpful.

4. Pose feedback as neutral questions to make your comments more palatable. This provides the artist opportunity to uncover his or her own flaws. I once hooked a rug where someone asked,

"Why is the crane so large?" I thought I had hooked a boat with a fisherman.

5. Don't send any indirect messages rejecting feedback you claim to be seeking. Unspoken messages are communicated through facial expressions (are you frowning?) and posture (are your arms crossed at the chest, and are you avoiding eye-contact?). Also, the way you ask for feedback may deter people from providing their opinions. "I think it's my best work. Tell me what you think," sends the message you seek only praise.

6. When seeking feedback, be specific. Ask a closed question (which requires a "yes" or "no" answer) specifying what you are trying to achieve. "I am trying to depict a sultry summer day. Does this rug achieve that?" Then encourage your responder to elaborate.

7. When providing feedback, try to employ the sandwich method. Begin with a positive comment. Then thoughtfully provide your ideas about what may not

work. Follow that up with another positive comment. For example, "Your rug radiates beautiful light. I wonder if more contrast might help distinguish the flower from the dog. Your shading of the dog's supper dish is effective."

IN CONCLUSION

Throughout *Hooked Rug Landscapes*, I have tried to provide tips, tricks, and rules to help in the design and execution of your own work. In addition, I have encouraged you to venture past the boundaries of established rules. In closing, let's look at a rug where the artist, MaryAnne Wise, has a deep understanding of traditional rules, and the artistic confidence and ability to break them in ways that result in an outstanding example of a hooked rug landscape.

This untitled piece reverses the notion of using color and value to depict a receding view. Here, the distant shore is hooked in warm colors that first attract

Stripes, 27" x 18", novelty fabrics, yarns, and ribbon on linen. Designed and hooked by Molly Dye, Jacksonville, Vermont, 2008.

Untitled, 52" x 32", #5-, 6-, and 7-cut over-dyed, hand-dyed, as-is, new, and recycled wool on monk's cloth. Designed and hooked by Mary Anne Wise, Stockholm, Wisconsin, 2007.

the eye. The foreground is hooked in cool, dulled-down colors. The juxtaposition of warm and cool, and near and far, lends a dreamlike quality to the overall composition. The view has a very interesting perspective. You are looking down a steep bank, to a distant scene. Note that the horses on the far shore are gigantic in proportion to the evergreen trees that line the shore. The stag and snow-covered pines in the foreground cast shadows in the snow. The water closest to

the viewer is of a darker value than the water that touches the far shore.

Be thoughtful in your choices. Respect your own instincts. Think about the dos and don'ts of rug hooking you have learned, and explore whether you should move on to a new level of artistic expression. Try to create pieces that evoke an emotional response. Honor your own artistic preferences. Take pleasure in the creation of each loop.

The Road, Norton Kansas Looking West, 26" x 18", #3-, 5-, and 7-cut hand-painted and hand-dyed wool on rug warp. Designed and hooked by Anne-Marie Littenberg, Burlington, Vermont, 2008.

Fifteen years ago, my husband and I embarked on what I call our Tall Grass Prairie vacation. We spent three weeks exploring two lane highways in Kansas, Missouri, and Colorado. It was August and hot, and I was completely in love with the vast vistas of road that unfurl through this beautiful part of the world. It was easy to imagine pioneers in covered wagons setting out for the west. There are places where you can still see ruts left in

the sod by their wagon wheels! We stopped at a motel in Norton, Kansas, where the beds were covered in chenille and the bath had those little, hard, paper-wrapped bars of soap. The room was spotlessly clean and cost $25. Our hosts were salt-of-the-earth, kind people. I was enchanted with how the road in Kansas rolled toward the rugged splendor of the Colorado Rocky Mountains. Cottonwood trees framed the vista.

Here are some of the tricks I used to help me hook this rug:

1. To enhance the sense that your road is receding, vary the size of your cuts of wool. I used a #7 cut in the first third (or closest part) of the road, a #5 in the middle third of the road, and a #3 cut for where the blacktop embraces the base of the mountains. The rest of the rug was hooked in a #3 cut.

2. Take advantage of the various effects you can achieve through

The Road, Norton Kansas Looking West (detail). I hooked the blacktop and yellow stripe using #7-cut wool in the foreground, #5-cut wool in the mid-ground, and #3-cut wool in the far-ground. This enhances the sense of the road receding into the distance. The yellow stripe is hooked as a straight line. The loops in the blacktop meander.

directional hooking. The prairie grass was hooked in the general direction of the movement of the road. The blacktop was hooked using a stitch that meanders, so each loop twists and turns in its own way. The foliage in the cottonwood was hooked in swirls. The sky is hooked in precise, vertical rows.

3. Experiment with the look you are trying to achieve. I wanted the color and value in this rug to resemble a watercolor. To create this look, I used only white Dorr wool. I did not use a wetting agent when I soaked the wool because I wanted to keep a white core. Also, I did not use salt in the dye pot because I did not want an even, consistent coloration of the wool. For each piece of wool, I had two pots simmering. One was the dye pot. I put in my dye mixture, and then threw in the white wool. The second pot simmered away on its own. This was the stop pot, and its purpose was to maintain the color exactly as I had it but also allow

the wool to cook sufficiently. When the white wool was the color and value I wanted, I yanked it out of the dye pot (regardless of how long it had been in the pot; often the wool is in the dye pot for only a moment or two) and moved it immediately to the stop pot where I quickly added citric acid to set the dye exactly as I wanted it. Note that I did not worry about keeping the wool in the first dye pot until the water ran clear. I let the wool finish cooking in the stop pot. I am not concerned about using all the dye in the pot. My priority is achieving the color, value, and clarity I want in the wool.

4. Use the same colors in multiple elements. The sky was dyed using very light formulations of all the major colors used in other elements of the rug. Thus, the sky has red, orange, green, yellow, blue, and lavender from the road, mountain, prairie grass, and cottonwood. The cottonwood has all the same colors as they sky, mountain, and road, but in much darker values.

To dye the sky, I mixed up high-acid, low-pigment formulations of the different colors. The dye formulas looked to be about the value and clarity of a fruit drink. I used an artist's paintbrush to apply the color to the wool, starting with the red. After applying each color, I thoroughly washed the paintbrush before moving on to the next color.

I knew I wanted the sky to have all the other colors from the rug. I was, however, uncertain of how to arrange those colors. Whenever I am uncertain of how to arrange colors so they appear to transition gradually, I turn to the rainbow and lay out my colors the way my second grade teacher taught me, after Roy G. Biv (red, orange, yellow, green, blue, indigo, violet).

To cook the sky, I laid a long sheet of tin foil over the piece of flat, painted wool and rolled it like a jelly roll so the layer of foil kept the different parts of the wool from touching each other. I pinched the ends of the foil to seal the packet and placed it in a 300-degree

The Road, Norton Kansas Looking West (detail). Blobs and swirls of closely colored wool in a range of subtle values suggest the undulations of a mountain.

oven for 40 minutes. When it was finished baking, I allowed it to cool and then gave it a quick wash with detergent and fabric softener in my washing machine, using the cold and hand-wash cycle. You could also easily and effectively use a spot or drag dye to achieve a beautiful sky.

5. Pay attention to the order in which you hook the strips. For the sky, I hooked the strips in the order in which they were cut from the wool. The big challenge in this type of hooking is to keep the strips in order. I have a board that has a piece of Velcro attached to it. I place the strips on the Velcro in the order they are cut from the wool. Then I place another strip of Velcro across the strips to secure them to the board.

The sky was the last part of the rug to be hooked. I hooked the sky vertically, from the top of the rug, all the way down to where the other loops for the distant mountain and treetop begin. You want to begin each strip in the exact same row that you began the previous strip for the sky. Pull a loop through every other hole in the rug warp. Place a strip of wool in every other row. Consistent, even loops are your goal. Do not trim any of your tails until you have completed hooking your sky and are satisfied with the placement of every loop.

Many of us learn that we should not hook with long strips. You will break this rule in creating your sky. Whatever the length is of the piece of wool you have painted, that is the length of the strips you will use to hook your sky.

Sometimes it can be difficult to tell which is the front or back of your wool strip after it has been cut. If you look carefully over the strip, you will see some areas that are of lighter value on one side than on the other. The side with the lighter splotches is the back. You want the wool on the visible side of your loops to come from the front of your painted sky wool.

6. Pay attention to proportions. Before you start hooking the sky, calculate the proportions of how much backing you will cover when your strip is fully hooked. For instance, I know in my hooking that the amount of backing I can expect to cover with a single strip is about 25 percent of the original length of the strip. We all hook differently, so calculate how much your strips reduce to help you assess how much wool you will need for the sky.

Feel free to interpret *The Road: Norton Kansas Looking West,* in any way that pleases you. Follow your own artistic instincts and create your own vision of a landscape.

Resources

American Folk Art and Craft Supply
Michele Stenson
1415 Hanover St., Rte. 139
Lower Level, Suite C
Hanover, MA 02339
781-871-7288
Over 100 hand-dyed colors, rug hook-
ing and braiding supplies

Angel Girl A Rug Hooking Studio
Victoria Jacobson
321 S. Main St.
Stillwater, MN 55082
612-741-2529
www.angelgirlstudio.com
angel_girl_rughooking@yahoo.com
Wool, classes, gifts, supplies and more

Appleton Krafts
152 Linebrook Rd.
Ipswich, MA 01938-2906
978-356-5878
www.appletonkrafts.biz
Gripper frames, gripper strips, superior
punch needle frames

Bolivar Cutters
Joan Bolivar
P. O. Box 539
Bridgewater, NS B4V 2X6
902-543-7762
www.bolivarcutter.com
Cutting machines

By the Door Hooked Rugs
Deanne Fitzpatrick
7 Electric St., RR5
Amherst, NS B4H 3Y3
800-328-7756
www.hookingrugs.com
Complete line of supplies, kits and
patterns

Cat House Rugs
Jyl Clark
415 W. First St.
New Albany, IN 47150
812-945-RUGS
www.cathouserugs.com
cathouserugs@iglou.com
Supplies, wool, patterns, kits, featuring
Kaye Miller Designs

Cross Creek Rug Studio
Beth Croup
13440 Taylor Wells Road
Chardon, OH 44024
440-635-0209

Cross Creek School
Cynthia Norwood
9334 Amberwood Dr.
Kirtland, OH 44094
440-256-3156
Workshops, Katherine Porter patterns.
By appointment only.

Emma Lou's Primitives
Emma Lou Lais
20614 W. 47th St.
Shawnee, KS 66218
913-745-5605
www.emmalousprimitives.com
Primitive rug patterns

Green Mountain Hooked Rugs, Inc.
Stephanie Ashworth-Krauss
2838 County Rd.
Montpelier, VT 05602
802-485-7274
www.GreenMountainHookedRugs.com
Patterns, supplies, and the annual
Green Mountain Rug School

Halcyon Yarn
12 School St.
Bath, ME 04530
800-341-0282
www.halcyonyarn.com
service@halcyonyarn.com
High quality rug yarn for finishing
hooked rugs

Harry M. Fraser Company
433 Duggins Rd.
Stoneville, NC 27048
336-573-9830
www.fraserrugs.com
fraserrugs@aol.com
Cloth-slitting machines, hooking and
braiding supplies

Hook Nook
Margaret Lutz
49 Samson Drive
Flemington, NJ 08822
908-806-8083
www.hook-nook.com
Lib Callaway rug patterns, hooking
supplies and instructions

Liziana Creations
Diana O'Brien
P. O. Box 310
Shelburne, MA 01370
Diana@galaxy.net
www.liziana.com
Supplies, backings, books, kits, wool,
patterns, designs, and more

Main Street Rugs
Melissa Elliott
311 S. Main St.
Versailles, KY 40383
859-879-0311
elliottky@yahoo.com

Meno Trigger Grip
Peggy Mineau
983 Union Lane
Little Suamico, WI 54141
920-826-2880
www.menotriggergrip.com
meno@new.rr.com

Moondance Color Company
622 Spencer Rd.
Oakham, MA 01068
508-882-3383
www.moondancecolor.com
Woolen fabrics, threads, patterns and
kits

Montpelier Arts Center
Roslyn Logsdon
9652 Muirkirk Rd.
Laurel, MD 20708
301-807-6261
roz.logsdon@verizon.net

New Earth Designs
Jeanne Benjamin
81 Lake Road
Brookfield, MA 01506
newearthdesigns@aliencamel.com
www.newearthdesigns.com
Patterns, dyed wool, swatches, and
yardages

Primitive Spirit
Karen Kahle
P. O. Box 1363
Eugene, OR 97440
541-344-4316
www.primitivespiritrugs.com
Patterns, dye books, dvds, catalogs

R & N Wool Studio.
Nancy Schell
P. O. Box 278
14413 Hwy 24
Woodland Park, CO 80866
719-687-2110
ricnan@netscape.com
Textures, solids, overdyed wool,
supplies, books, patterns, kits

The Red Saltbox
Wendy Miller
The Robinson House
503 S. Brady St.
Attica, IN 47918
765-762-6292
www.theredsaltbox.com
Wide-cuts, textured wools, custom
workshops, dye books, swatches,
catalogs

Rigby Cutters
P. O. Box 158, Dept. RH
249 Portland Rd.
Bridgton, ME 04009
207-647-5679
Cloth-stripping machines

Rittermere-Hurst-Field
P. O. Box 487
Aurora, ON L4G 3L6
800-268-9813
www.LetsHookRugs.com

Ruckman Mill Farm
Susan Feller
P. O. Box 409
Augusta, WV 26704
304-496-8073
www.RuckmanMillFarm.com
Susan Feller's rug designs

Rug Art and Supply
Shelley Flannery and Barbara Hanson
3037 NE Brogden
Hillsboro, OR 97124
503-648-3979
shelley-barbara@rugartsupply.com
www.rugartsupply.com
Wool, supplies, Townsend Cutters,
Nancy Miller hooks, frames, kits

Rug Hooking Magazine
5067 Ritter Road
Mechanicsburg, PA 17055
717-796-0411
www.rughookingmagazine.com

Spruce Ridge Studio
Kris Miller
1786 Eager Rd.
Howell, MI 48855
517-546-7732
kris@spruceridgestudios.com
www.spruceridgestudios.com
Patterns, kits, books and supplies

Spruce Top Rug Hooking Studio
Carol Harvey-Clark
255 W. Main St.
Mahone Bay, NS B0J 2E0
888-RUG-HOOK
www.sprucetoprughookingstudio.com

The Wool Basket
Karen Haskett
526 N. Cleveland Ave.
Loveland, CO 80537
970-203-0999
Karen@thewoolbasket.com
www.thewoolbasket.com

The Wool Studio
Rebecca Erb
706 Brownsville Rd.
Sinking Spring, PA 19608
610-678-5448
www.thewoolstudio.com
thewoolstudio@comcast.net
Quality woolens, specializing in
textures for the primitive rug hooker

Townsend Industries, Inc.
P. O. Box 97
Altoona, IA 50009
877-868-3544
www.townsendindustries.com
info@townsendindustries.com
Fabric cutters, frames

W. Cushing and Company
21 North St., Box 351
Kennebunkport, ME 04046
207-967-3711
www.wcushing.com
customer@wcushing.com
Joan Moshimer's rug hooking studio,
Cushing Perfection dyes, Pearl
McGown patterns, rug hooking
supplies

Whispering Hill Farm
Donna Swanson
Box 186, Rte. 169
S. Woodstock, CT 06267
860-928-0162
www.whispering-hill.com
whisperhill@earthlink.net
Complete rug hooking supplier: wool,
hooks, patterns, backings, books,
frames, cutters.